PASTISSIMA!
Pasta the Italian Way

PASTISSIMA!
Pasta the Italian Way

Text by Leonardo Castellucci
Photography by Marco Lanza
Set Design by Cinzia Calamai

TIME-LIFE BOOKS IS A DIVISION OF TIME LIFE INC.
TIME-LIFE CUSTOM PUBLISHING

Vice President and Publisher	Terry Newell
Associate Publisher	Teresa Hartnett
Vice President of Sales and Marketing	Neil Levin
Director of New Product Development	Quentin McAndrew
Director of Special Sales	Liz Ziehl

TIME-LIFE is a trademark of Time Warner Inc. U.S.A.

Library of Congress Cataloging-in-Publication Data
Pastissima! : pasta the Italian way
    p.   cm. -- (Pane & vino)
    Includes index.
    ISBN 0-7835-4942-3
    I. Cookery (Pasta)   2. Cookery, Italian.   I. Time-Life Books.   II. Series.
TX801.V468 1998
641.8'22--dc21   97-1823
                                                       CIP

© McRae Books 1996
Conceived, edited and designed by McRae Books, Florence, Italy
Text: Leonardo Castellucci
Photography: Marco Lanza
Set Design: Cinzia Calamai
Design: Marco Nardi

Translation from the Italian and adaptation:
Anne McRae
Editing: Alison Leach
Illustrations: Alessandro Baldanzi

The Publishers would like to thank Mastro Ciliegia (Fiesole), Pasquinucci
(Florence), La Boutique della pasta fresca (Florence), Casa pulita (Florence),
for their assistance during the production of this book

Color separations: Fotolito Toscana, Florence, Italy
Printed and bound in Italy by Grafiche Editoriali Padane, Cremona

Other titles in the same series:
Verdure! Vegetables the Italian Way
Antipasti! Appetizers the Italian Way
Zuppe, Risotto e Polenta! Italian Soup, Risotto and Polenta Dishes

CONTENTS

Introduction 6-7

A Short History of Pasta 8-9

Pasta Basics 10-35
Types of Pasta ~ Ingredients
Utensils ~ Basic Sauces

Dried Pasta 36-63

Fresh Pasta 64-77

Filled Pasta 78-91

Baked Pasta 92-103

Gnocchi 104-113

Soups and Salads 114-119

Making Fresh Pasta

at Home 120-123

Index 124-127

INTRODUCTION

In Italy there are entire encyclopedias devoted to pasta cookery, and our biggest challenge here was how to squeeze such a wealth of knowledge into one quite modest volume while still conveying something of the breadth of the subject. The solution seemed to be to create a book that can be used in two different ways; first as a simple set of pasta recipes, and these you will find in the main part of the book (pp.36–119), and, second, "interactively", by providing a series of basic sauces, tips on types of pasta to serve them with, and instructions on making pasta at home. By combining pasta and sauces in different ways you will be able create a wide variety of dishes. Italians are famous (or notorious) throughout the world for being creative and "flexible." This same flexibility can, and should, be brought to Italian cooking. Don't cancel the dinner party if you can't find pancetta (use bacon), gorgonzola (blue vein with a dash of fresh cream?), or fresh rosemary (try dried). The results will be different, but the important thing is to enjoy the food, both eating it and preparing it. Buon appetito!

A Short History of Pasta

Like many things, the origins of pasta are lost in the mists of prehistory. We can only assume that it was "invented" some time after our ancestors had learned to cultivate cereals and to grind them into flour. The earliest references to pasta on the Italian peninsula date from Etruscan times, before the Romans and contemporary with the ancient Greeks. An Etruscan tomb at Cerveteri, in Tuscany, has murals with images of knives, a rolling pin, and an object that looks very similar to our modern wheel cutter, the one used for giving fluted edges to fresh pasta, such as pappardelle or tagliatelle.

Etruscan bas-relief dating from the 4th century B.C. Cerveteri, Central Itay.

In Ancient Rome it seems that only the wealthiest citizens could afford to eat pasta. In his cookbook Apician, chef to the rich and famous of Rome, gives recipes for several dishes made with *lagane*, which was what the Romans called fresh pasta.

After the fall of Rome all traces of pasta vanished for several centuries.

At the beginning of the 12th century an Arab writer, Abu Abdallah Muhammad Idris, in a book destined for the Norman king of Sicily, Roger II, gives a very precise description of how to dry, and thus preserve, fresh pasta. When the Sicilians had learned how to conserve this delicious food, they wasted no time in letting the mainlanders in on the secret. In Naples, Amalfi, Genoa, and many other port towns, the manufacture and sale of pasta soon became a roaring trade.

Even so, these early "Italians" (remember that the country wasn't united, and thus really "Italy" until 1870) had rather different ideas about how pasta should be served than the ones you will find in this book. Pasta was usually cooked in milk or broth and served with sugar, cheese, butter, and sweet spices. It wasn't until the 18th century that some sort of order was established in culinary habits, and sweet and savory dishes were distinguished. From that time on pasta began to be served more or less as it is today, with sauces based on tomatoes, meat, and vegetables.

In the second half of this century, as Italy moved from being a poverty-stricken exporter of migrant labor to a major industrial power, new and sophisticated machines were invented, and pasta is now manufactured throughout the peninsula and exported all over the world. Which brings a tip to mind; when buying pasta, always try to find an Italian-made brand. This is not exaggerated nationalism, nor are we in the pay of any local manufacturers, it's just that the combination of Italian flour, Italian water, and Italian know-how makes superior quality pasta!

DRIED PASTA

The number and variety of pasta shapes available is bewildering. Over the years any special occasion or celebration has been a good excuse to invent a new one! Add to this the fact that the same pasta shape may change its name from region to region, and the different pasta manufacturers may call the same pasta shape by different names, and you will begin to understand why you need to approach the subject with some general guidelines in mind.

The long and short pasta shapes on this page are store-bought and made from dried hard wheat flour and water, while the smaller soup pasta shapes may also be made from egg and soft wheat flour.

LONG AND SHORT PASTA

All dried pasta can be divided into long or short shapes. The longer ones should be served with oil-based sauces that cling to their shapes, while many of the short pasta shapes are good with chunkier sauces that can be scooped up with the fork.

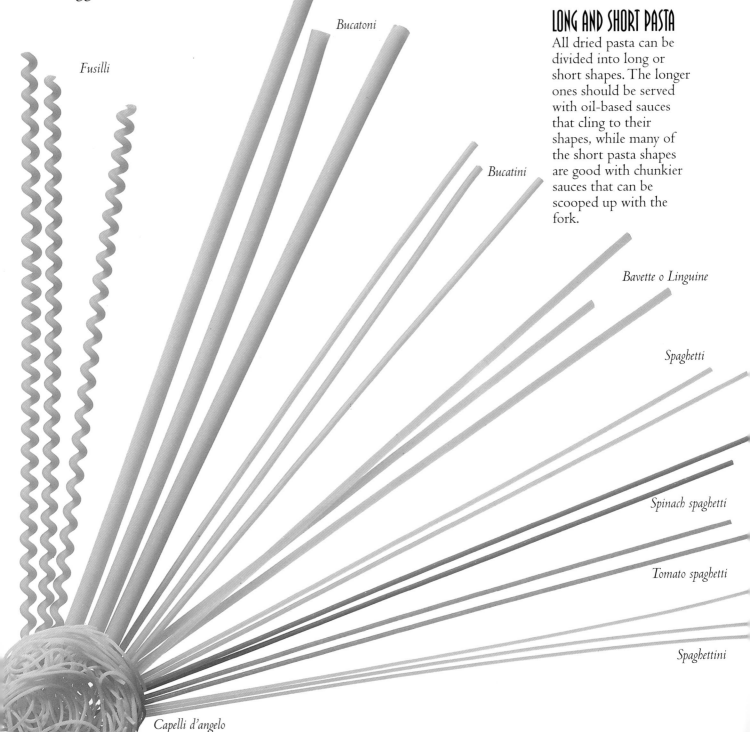

Bucatoni

Fusilli

Bucatini

Bavette o Linguine

Spaghetti

Spinach spaghetti

Tomato spaghetti

Spaghettini

Capelli d'angelo

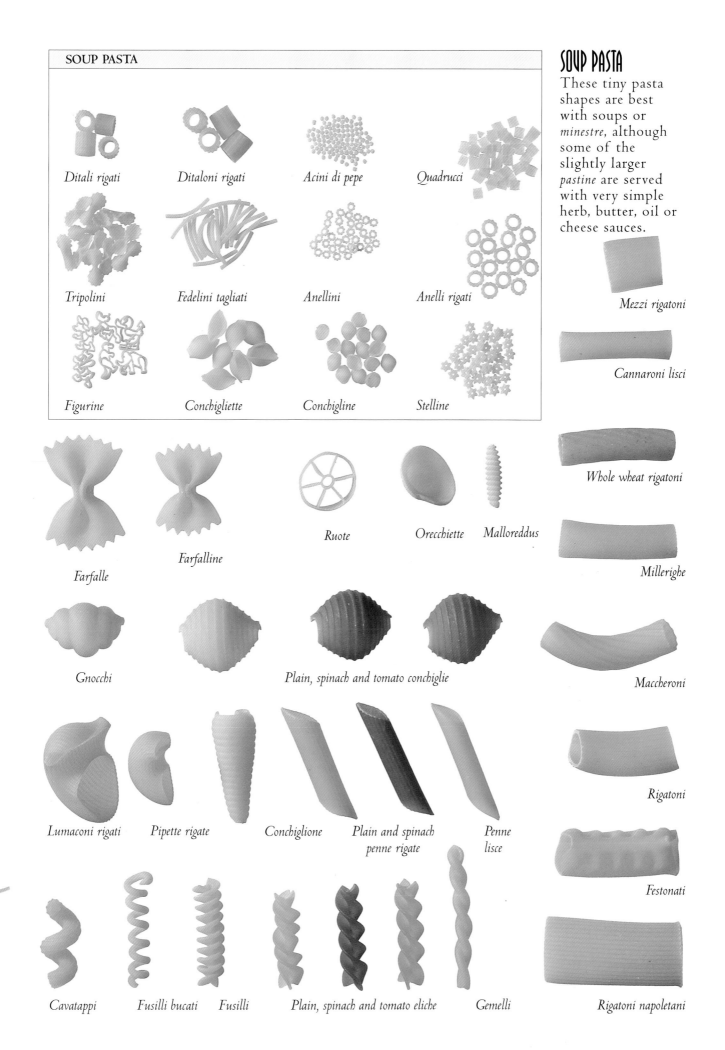

SOUP PASTA

Ditali rigati Ditaloni rigati Acini di pepe Quadrucci

Tripolini Fedelini tagliati Anellini Anelli rigati

Figurine Conchigliette Conchigline Stelline

Farfalle Farfalline Ruote Orecchiette Malloreddus

Gnocchi Plain, spinach and tomato conchiglie

Lumaconi rigati Pipette rigate Conchiglione Plain and spinach penne rigate Penne lisce

Cavatappi Fusilli bucati Fusilli Plain, spinach and tomato eliche Gemelli

SOUP PASTA

These tiny pasta shapes are best with soups or *minestre*, although some of the slightly larger *pastine* are served with very simple herb, butter, oil or cheese sauces.

Mezzi rigatoni

Cannaroni lisci

Whole wheat rigatoni

Millerighe

Maccheroni

Rigatoni

Festonati

Rigatoni napoletani

Fresh and Filled Pasta

By fresh pasta I mean pasta made from egg and soft-wheat flour, although the term "fresh" is somewhat misleading, since egg pasta can also be dried. In fact you will find that commercially made, dried tagliatelle, fettuccine, pappardelle, and others, are often a better (and certainly more economical) alternative to the refrigerated "fresh" pasta available in supermarkets and specialty stores. However, the best fresh pasta you can get is the homemade variety. If you have the time, and a little patience, the results will be better than anything you can buy. The added bonus is that making pasta is a very satisfying experience. See instructions on pp. 120-123. As with dried, store-bought pasta, the names and shapes of fresh and filled pasta types vary from region to region in Italy. These are a selection of the most common types, in their most usual shapes, and sporting their more recurrent names.

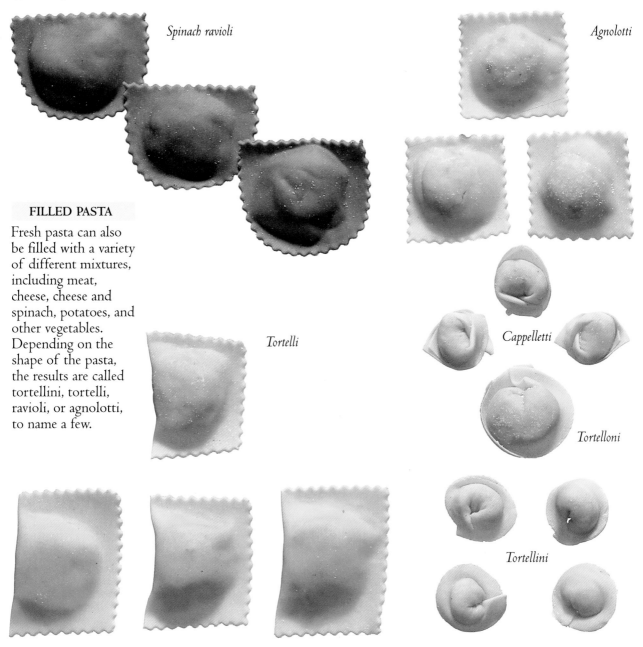

Spinach ravioli

Agnolotti

FILLED PASTA

Fresh pasta can also be filled with a variety of different mixtures, including meat, cheese, cheese and spinach, potatoes, and other vegetables. Depending on the shape of the pasta, the results are called tortellini, tortelli, ravioli, or agnolotti, to name a few.

Tortelli

Cappelletti

Tortelloni

Tortellini

Pappardelle

Tagliolini

Fettuccine

Paglia e fieno

Tagliatelle

Maltagliati

Serving Suggestions
High quality fresh
and filled pasta are
good with simple
butter, cream, or
butter and herb
sauces, well sprinkled
with freshly grated
parmesan cheese.
These simple sauces
should highlight the
delicate taste of the
egg pasta without
camouflaging it.
Mushroom, truffle,
asparagus, and walnut
sauces are also good.
Other traditional
recipes include sauces
based on wild game,
such as duck, wild
boar, or rabbit, as well
as tasty, well-cooked
lamb and veal.

Lasagne

GNOCCHI

Strictly speaking gnocchi are not pasta. In Italy preliminaries to a main course will consist of one or more *antipasti* (appetizers), followed by a *primo piatto* (first course). Pasta dishes are a typical first course but there are also many others, such as risotto, polenta, zuppe, and gnocchi. Gnocchi have been included here because they are so good, and also because they are quite easy to make at home, even for beginners.

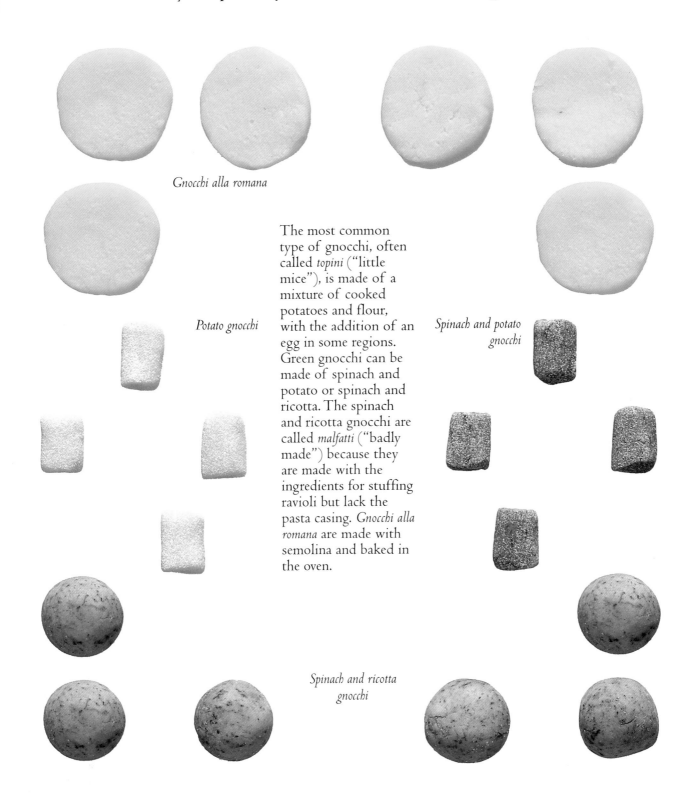

Gnocchi alla romana

Potato gnocchi

Spinach and potato gnocchi

The most common type of gnocchi, often called *topini* ("little mice"), is made of a mixture of cooked potatoes and flour, with the addition of an egg in some regions. Green gnocchi can be made of spinach and potato or spinach and ricotta. The spinach and ricotta gnocchi are called *malfatti* ("badly made") because they are made with the ingredients for stuffing ravioli but lack the pasta casing. *Gnocchi alla romana* are made with semolina and baked in the oven.

Spinach and ricotta gnocchi

SPECIAL PASTA

In recent years there has been an explosion in the number of colored and flavored pasta available. The purists are shocked, and I suspect that it is the tourists who are buying up most of these innovative varieties, particularly since they are sold in and around the chic, central streets of Rome and Florence, and are also widely available in souvenir shops in Tuscan hill towns. In any case, colored pasta is fun and pretty to look at!

These are just some of the new colors and flavors available:

1 Plain
2 Basil
3 Beet
4 Carrot
5 Mountain herb
6 Porcini mushroom
7 Saffron
8 Squid's ink
9 Spinach
10 Salmon
11 Whole wheat
12 Tomato

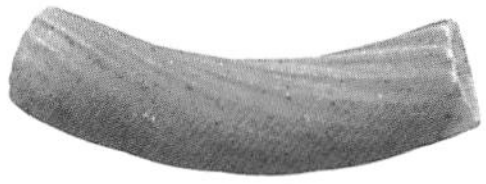

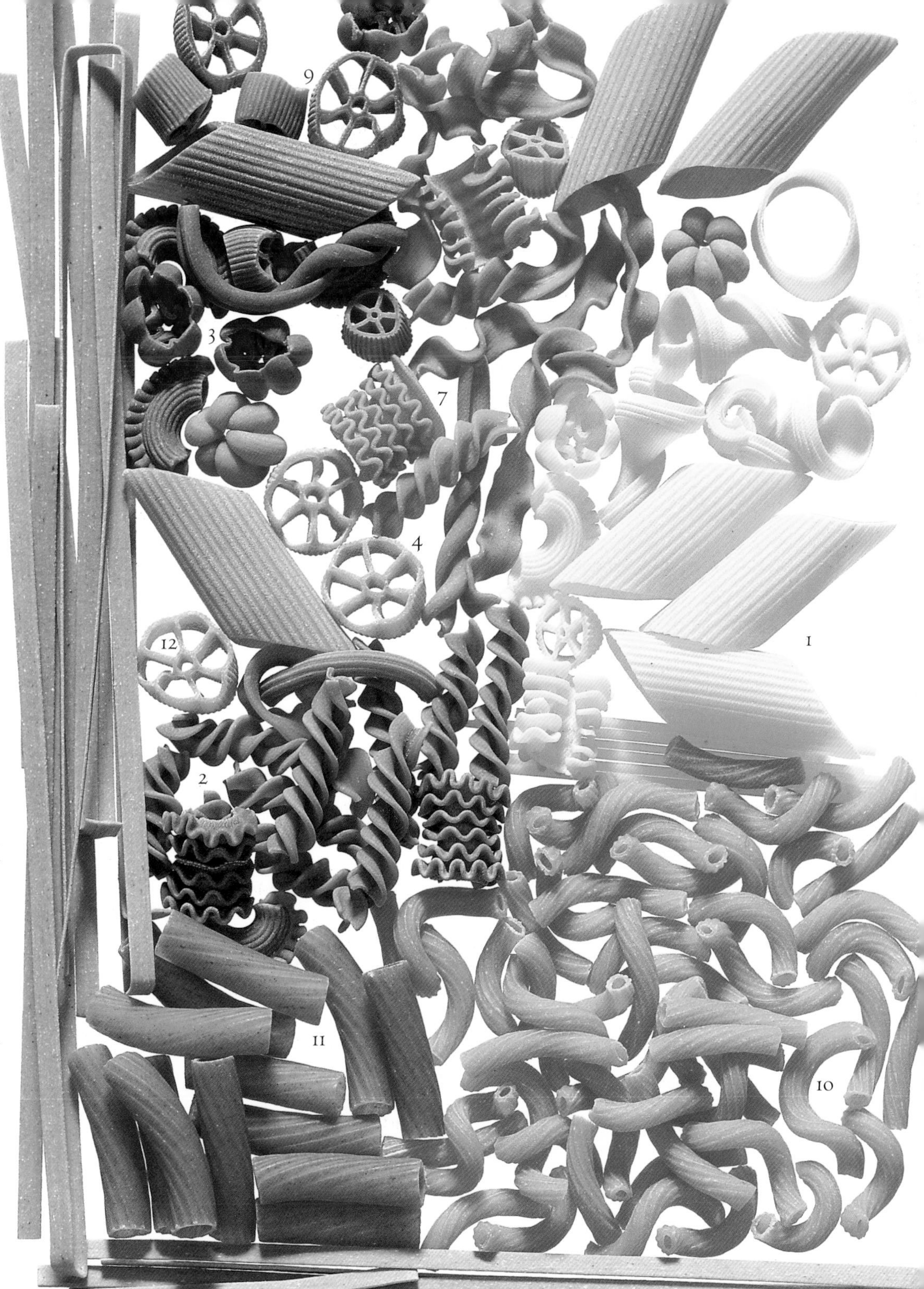

Oil, Cheese and Other Ingredients

Many ingredients of classic pasta cookery, like butter, tomatoes, and onions, are common throughout the world and need little introduction. Others, some of which are shown below, are more specific to the Italian pantry and may require some explanation.

OLIVE OIL

Olive oil is a fundamental ingredient in almost all pasta dishes and should be chosen with care. Buy only the highest quality oil, which is always labelled *"extra-vergine."*

Don't economize on olive oil or use other vegetable oils in its place, even for cooking. If you are on a low-fat diet, you may want to reduce the quantity of oil in the recipes a little.

WINE

Some purists still insist that wine should never be served with pasta. As you will have noticed if you have ever been to Italy, this line of thought is seriously endangered. Throughout this book I have suggested a type of wine (dry, red, white, sparkling) for most recipes. I have also suggested an Italian wine which I think will go well with the dish. These are guidelines only, and you should follow your own preferences entirely.

Meats

MORTADELLA
Mortadella is a kind of sausage made of lean pork cooked slowly to develop its special subtle blend of flavors. The best mortadella comes from Bologna and it is used in many Bolognese specialties (see tortellini, Bolognese meat sauce).

PANCETTA
Pancetta is made of pork and is comparable to an unsmoked form of bacon.

PROSCIUTTO
Prosciutto is a form of ham which has been salted and air-cured. The best kind is cured naturally over quite long periods of time (up to a year). It is never smoked.

Cheeses

Among the hundreds of Italian cheeses, only a few are used often in pasta cooking. These (either Italian imports or locally made brands) are now widely available outside of Italy.

FONTINA
Fontina is made of cow's milk and comes from the alpine areas of northwest Italy. It is ideal for melting over baked pasta dishes.

PECORINO
Pecorino cheese is made of ewe's milk. The best pecorino for grating over pasta is called *pecorino romano*, which has a sharp and pungent taste. Like parmesan, it should be bought in a wedge and grated as required.

PARMIGIANO
Parmesan is made of skimmed cow's milk and carefully aged for at least 18 months before use. If you can, try real Italian *parmigiano-reggiano* at least once; you will at least discover what parmesan should taste like. If you are buying parmesan in a good specialty store, a wedge will be cut from the wheel as you watch. Never buy the grated varieties; always grate it yourself as you need it.

GORGONZOLA
Gorgonzola, a specialty of northern Italy made from cow's milk, makes a wonderfully creamy pasta sauce when melted with a little butter or cream.

RICOTTA
Fresh ricotta has a deliciously light and delicate flavor. It forms the basis of many stuffings for filled pasta. Buy it in a good Italian deli or specialty cheese store. Try to avoid ricotta sold in plastic containers, which bears very little resemblance to the real thing.

MOZZARELLA
Real mozzarella cheese is made from water buffalo milk, which is creamier and tastier than cow's milk. However, since it is expensive and not always easy to find outside of Italy, you will probably have to settle for mozzarella made from the milk of cows. If it is fresh and a good brand, this will be just as satisfying.

HERBS AND SPICES

There are a limited number of fairly common herbs and spices that are essential in pasta cookery. It goes without saying that fresh herbs and freshly ground spices will always produce superior results to dried or powdered ones. However, fresh herbs may not always be available and in that case you should use dried ones. All herbs and spices in powdered form are to be shunned.

ORIGANO
Oregano is closely related to marjoram, but has a much stronger flavor. It is one of the few herbs that dries well, so don't worry too much if you can't get it fresh.

CAPPERI
Capers are the unopened buds of a flowering plant that grows wild on Mediterranean hillsides. They can be bought either pickled in vinegar or packed in salt. The pickled variety keeps well in the refrigerator.

PEPE NERO
Black pepper should be bought as whole peppercorns. Grind them over your sauce or dish as required.

AGLIO
Garlic is one of the basic ingredients of most pasta sauces. Always use fresh cloves, either whole or chopped. When sautéing garlic take care that it never gets past a light gold color or it will produce a very acrid flavor that will taint the whole dish.

PEPERONCINO
Small red hot chilies are widely available throughout Italy. They keep indefinitely in an airtight jar so if you are ever in Italy, stock up on the real thing. Otherwise crushed dried chilies will be a good substitute.

ALLORO
Bay leaves are richly aromatic and are generally added whole to sauces during the cooking and removed before serving. They dry well and, stored in an airtight jar, will keep indefinitely.

NOCE MOSCATA
Buy whole nutmegs and store them in an airtight jar. Use a fine grater to grate the nutmeg as you need it.

PREZZEMOLO

Parsley is one of the basic herbs in pasta cookery. Italian parsley is the continental flat-leaf variety shown here. It has a different flavor from common curly-leaf parsley and will produce more authentic results. However since parsley doesn't dry well, I would prefer fresh curly-leaf parsley to dried flat-leaf.

MAGGIORANA

Marjoram's spicy aroma is delicious with fish- and vegetable-based sauces. It doesn't dry well and should always be used fresh.

BASILICO

Basil combines very well with tomato. For full flavor, the leaves should be torn rather than chopped and added to the sauce just before removing from heat.

SALVIA

Sage is best fresh, but if you are using it in its dried form, use about half the amount given in the recipes since it becomes so much more potent when dry.

ROSMARINO

Rosemary is a common herb in Italian cooking and usually associated with roasts. Its finely chopped fresh leaves will also enliven meat- and fish-based sauces.

Utensils for Making and Cooking Pasta

Most well stocked kitchens will already have much of the basic equipment for preparing and serving pasta. If you need extra pieces they will be easy to find in kitchen-supply stores. If you can, always choose good quality equipment. It will last longer and the results will be better.

POT
Large capacity pot with a close-fitting lid.

PASTA MACHINE
This is a basic hand-cranked pasta machine. Electric versions are also available.

SKILLET
Heavy, shallow-sided pan in aluminum, stainless steel, or cast iron.

SAUCEPAN
Versatile pans in several sizes.

WHEEL CUTTER
To give fluted edges when cutting fresh pasta.

CUTTING BOARD
Heavy duty board for cutting and slicing vegetables and meat.

SAUTÉ PAN
Deep-sided pan, large enough to hold the pasta and sauce together.

METAL TONGS
For picking up or serving spaghetti.

WOODEN SPOON
AND FORK
For stirring pasta and sauces.

COLANDER
Large metal colander for draining pasta.

CHEESE GRATER
Choose the rounded stainless steel grater specially designed for parmesan and other cheeses.

MEASURING CUP
Cup with liquid and dry measurements.

FOOD PROCESSOR
For chopping, shredding, and puréeing ingredients for sauces.

FOOD MILL
Hand-cranked mill for puréeing ingredients for filled pasta stuffings and other ingredients for sauces.

BAKING DISH
Large, rectangular, ovenproof baking dish for baked pasta.

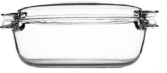

ROLLING PIN
A pasta rolling pin is longer and thinner than the normal one.

SLOTTED SPOON
Used for removing gnocchi from the pan and for skimming broth.

TIPS FOR COOKING PASTA

TIMING
One of the most difficult things for the novice pasta cook is knowing when the pasta is cooked. It should be boiled until the outer layers are soft enough to absorb the delicious sauce you have prepared, while the inside is firm enough to pose some resistance to the bite. This is called *al dente*.

WATER
Pasta needs lots of water to cook properly. Allow about 4 quarts for each pound of pasta. Never cook even a small amount of pasta in less than 3 quarts.

SALT
Allow at least 1 heaped tablespoon of salt for each pound of pasta. Add the salt after the water has come to a boil, just before adding the pasta.

QUANTITY
As a general guideline, allow about 4 ounces per head. If the pasta is a first course between antipasti and the main, you may need less. If you are just serving pasta with a salad, you may need more.

COOKING
When the water is boiling, add all the pasta at once. Stir with a wooden spoon so it doesn't stick together. Cover the pot with a lid and bring it back to a boil as soon as possible. When the water is boiling again, leave to cook uncovered, stirring frequently.

DRAINING
Drain the pasta in a colander as soon as it is cooked. Don't leave it sitting in the water as it will get mushy and overcooked.

SERVING
Pasta should be served immediately. If it is left sitting, it will turn into a sticky lump.

Basic Sauces

This section features recipes for 14 basic sauces and suggestions for the best types of pasta with which to serve them.

Salsa al pomodoro
Simple tomato sauce

Oil-based tomato sauce goes well with all dried, hard wheat pasta, such as spaghetti, spaghettini, penne, bucatini, and fusilli. It is also good with spinach and whole wheat pasta.

Serves: 6; Preparation: 15 minutes; Cooking: 20 minutes; Level of difficulty: Simple

Put the garlic and oil in a heavy-bottomed skillet and sauté over medium heat until the garlic is golden brown. § Add the basil and tomatoes. Season with salt and pepper, and simmer for about 15-20 minutes, or until the oil begins to separate from the tomato.

§ Cook the pasta in a large pot of salted, boiling water until *al dente*. Drain well and transfer to a heated serving dish. Toss well with the sauce and serve at once.

Variations
– Sauté 1 small onion, 1 carrot, 1 stalk celery, and 1 tablespoon parsley, all finely chopped, with the garlic.
– Add ½ teaspoon crushed chilies.
– Crumble 4 anchovy fillets into the sauce with the tomatoes.
– Add 2 tablespoons small salted capers.

■ INGREDIENTS
- 4 cloves garlic, finely chopped
- 6 tablespoons extra-virgin olive oil
- 3 tablespoons torn fresh basil leaves
- 5 cups peeled and chopped fresh or canned tomatoes
- salt and freshly ground black pepper
- 1¼ pounds dried pasta

Salsa di burro e pomodoro
Tomato and butter sauce

This sauce is delicious with all types of fresh pasta and gnocchi.

Serves 4; Preparation: 10 minutes; Cooking: 30 minutes; Level of difficulty: Simple

Combine the garlic and onion in a skillet with the butter and oil. Sauté over medium heat until the onion is transparent. § Add the tomatoes and season with salt and pepper. Simmer over medium-low heat for about 25 minutes. Add the basil just before removing from heat.

§ Cook the pasta in a large pot of salted, boiling water until *al dente*. Drain and place in a heated serving dish. Pour the sauce over the top and toss gently until well mixed. Serve hot with lots of parmesan for sprinkling over each portion.

Variation
– Stir 1½ cups fresh cream into the sauce after removing from heat for a *rosé* or pink sauce.

■ INGREDIENTS
- 2 cloves garlic, finely chopped
- 1 large onion, very finely chopped
- ¼ cup butter
- 2 tablespoons extra-virgin olive oil
- 3 cups peeled and chopped fresh or canned tomatoes
- 6 fresh basil leaves, torn
- salt and freshly ground black pepper
- 14 ounces fresh pasta

Right:
Spaghetti con salsa al pomodoro

BALSAMELLA
Béchamel sauce

Béchamel is an essential ingredient in many filled and baked pasta dishes. It can also be used to revive leftover pasta by simply tossing the pasta and béchamel for 2–3 minutes in a pan over medium heat or baking together in a hot oven for about 15 minutes. Béchamel is simple and quick to make and should be used as soon as it is made.

Makes: about 3 cups; Preparation & Cooking: 10 minutes; Level of difficulty: Simple

Heat the milk in a saucepan until it is almost boiling. § Melt the butter in a heavy-bottomed pan over low heat. Add the flour gradually and stir until smooth. § Remove from heat and add the milk a few tablespoons at a time, stirring constantly. When all the milk has been added, season with salt and return to low heat. Cook for 3-4 minutes, or until the sauce is thick, stirring all the time. If any lumps form, beat the sauce rapidly with a fork or hand whisk until they dissolve.

■ INGREDIENTS

• 3 cups milk
• ⅓ cup butter
• ⅔ cup sifted all-purpose flour
• salt

SALSA DI BURRO E PARMIGIANO
Butter and parmesan sauce

Freshly grated parmesan tossed with hot pasta and high quality butter is always delicious. It is served with all types of dried, fresh and filled pasta, both store-bought and homemade.

Serves: 4; Preparation & Cooking: 5 minutes; Level of difficulty: Simple

Cook the pasta in a large pot of salted, boiling water until *al dente*. Drain and transfer to a heated serving dish. § Add half the cheese and toss well until it melts creamily over the pasta. Add the butter and remaining cheese and continue to toss until the butter has melted. Serve hot.

■ INGREDIENTS

• 1½ cups freshly grated parmesan cheese
• ½ cup fresh, high quality butter, chopped (not straight from the refrigerator)
• 14 ounces pasta

SALSA DI BURRO E SALVIA
Butter and sage sauce

The clean, fuzzy taste of fresh sage and butter combines well with fresh pasta and gnocchi.

Preparation & Cooking: 5 minutes; Level of difficulty: Simple

Put the butter and sage in a heavy-bottomed pan over low heat and leave until the butter turns light gold.
§ Cook the pasta in a large pot of salted, boiling water until *al dente*. Drain well and transfer to a preheated serving dish. Pour the sauce over the pasta. Toss well, sprinkle with the parmesan and serve at once.

■ INGREDIENTS

• ½ cup fresh, high quality butter
• 9 fresh sage leaves, torn
• 4 tablespoons freshly grated parmesan cheese
• 14 ounces fresh or filled pasta, or potato gnocchi

Right:
Preparing béchmal sauce

Ragù di carne alla bolognese
Bolognese meat sauce

The secret of a successful ragù lies in the cooking; it should be simmered over a low heat for at least 2½ hours. It can be made ahead and kept in the refrigerator for up to 3 days, or frozen. Ragù is very versatile and can be served with most dried pasta shapes, with fresh, long pasta, such as tagliatelle, with many filled pasta dishes, and with potato and spinach gnocchi.

Serves: 6; Preparation: 30 minutes; Cooking: 3 hours; Level of difficulty: Simple

Combine the pancetta, onion, celery, and carrot in a sauté pan with the butter and cook over medium heat until the onion is light gold in color. § Add the beef, pork, and sausage and cook until the mixture is all the same color. Add the clove, cinnamon, and pepper. Stir in the tomatoes and continue to cook over medium heat for 15 minutes. § Add the milk and season with salt. Turn the heat down to low and simmer for at least 2½ hours, stirring from time to time.

§ Cook the pasta in a large pot of salted, boiling water until *al dente*. Drain well and toss with the meat sauce. Serve hot.

■ INGREDIENTS

- ¾ cup diced pancetta
- 1 large onion, 1 stalk celery, 1 medium carrot, all finely chopped
- ⅓ cup butter
- 12 ounces ground beef
- 4 ounces ground pork
- 3 ounces Italian pork sausage, skinned and crumbled
- 1 freshly ground clove
- dash of cinnamon
- ⅓ teaspoon freshly ground black pepper
- 2 14-ounce cans chopped tomatoes
- 1½ cups milk
- salt
- 1¼ pounds dried, fresh, or filled pasta or gnocchi

Sugo di carne veloce
Quick meat sauce

Serves: 4; Preparation: 20 minutes; Cooking: 30 minutes; Level of difficulty: Simple

Soak the mushrooms in a bowl of tepid water for 20 minutes. Rinse well and chop coarsely. § Put the onion, garlic, pancetta, and oil in a skillet and sauté over medium heat until the onion is transparent. Add the sausage and sauté for 5 more minutes. § Add the tomatoes and mushrooms, season with salt and pepper, and simmer over medium low heat for about 20 minutes, stirring frequently.

§ Cook the pasta in a large pot of salted, boiling water until *al dente*. Drain and transfer to a heated serving dish. Toss well with the sauce and serve hot.

■ INGREDIENTS

- 2 ounces dried porcini mushrooms
- 2 medium onions, finely chopped
- 2 cloves garlic, finely chopped
- 1 cup diced pancetta
- 4 tablespoons extra-virgin olive oil
- 14 ounces Italian pork sausage, skinned and crumbled
- 2 14-ounce cans chopped tomatoes
- salt and freshly ground black pepper
- 14 ounces dried or fresh pasta or gnocchi

Right: Tortellini al ragù di carne alla bolognese

Pesto alla genovese
Genoese Basil Sauce

Pesto comes from the Liguria region in northern Italy and is named for its capital city Genoa. Traditionally it is served with trenette, a local egg-based pasta similar to fettuccine. It is also good with dried pasta, particularly the long shapes (spaghetti, spaghettini, linguine), and is delicious with potato gnocchi.

Serves: 4; Preparation: 10 minutes; Level of difficulty: Simple

Combine the basil, pine nuts, garlic, olive oil, and salt in a food processor and chop until smooth. Place mixture in a large serving bowl and stir in the cheeses.

§ Cook the pasta in a pot of salted, boiling water until *al dente*. Drain well and transfer to a heated serving dish. Add 2 tablespoons of the water from the pasta pot and a knob of butter. Toss vigorously with the pesto and serve hot.

VARIATION
– Add 2 tablespoons fresh ricotta cheese just before serving for a richer sauce.

■ INGREDIENTS

- 3 cups fresh basil leaves
- 3 tablespoons pine nuts
- 2 cloves garlic
- ¾ cup extra-virgin olive oil
- salt
- 3 tablespoons grated parmesan cheese
- 3 tablespoons grated pecorino cheese
- knob of butter for serving
- 14 ounces pasta

Pesto toscano
Tuscan-style pesto

This recipe is an up-dated version of one said to have been developed by the chefs of the Medici family in Florence in the 16th century. It can be served with most long and short dried pasta shapes.

Serves: 4; Preparation: 10 minutes; Level of difficulty: Simple

Put the walnuts, basil, and garlic in a food processor and chop to a cream. Transfer to a mixing bowl. § Remove the crust from the bread roll and soak the inside in the broth. Squeeze well and add to the walnut mixture. Add salt to taste, lemon juice, and oil (you may need slightly more or slightly less oil depending on how much the walnuts absorb), and mix well.

§ Cook the pasta in a large pot of salted, boiling water until *al dente*. Drain and transfer to a heated serving dish. Toss well with the sauce and serve hot.

■ INGREDIENTS

- 30 shelled walnuts
- ¾ cup fresh basil leaves
- 1½ cloves garlic
- 1 large bread roll
- 1½ cups meat broth (see recipe p. 34)
- salt
- juice of 1 lemon
- 3 tablespoons extra-virgin olive oil
- 14 ounces pasta

Right:
Linguine al pesto

Intingolo di funghi porcini
Italian mushroom sauce

Fresh porcini mushrooms are hard to find outside of Italy and France but they are widely available in their dried form. If you can't get fresh porcini, combine a small amount of soaked, dried porcini with fresh white mushrooms. The dried porcini have such a strong musky taste they will flavor your dish almost as well as the fresh ones. Mushroom sauce is very good with fresh pasta (tagliolini, fettuccine, tagliatelle, pappardelle) and also with long dried pasta shapes (spaghetti, bucatini, etc.). Try replacing the meat sauce in Lasagne al forno *(see recipe p. 94) with 1 quantity of this sauce.*

Serves: 4; Preparation: 10 minutes + time to soak the mushrooms; Cooking: 30 minutes; Level of difficulty: Simple

If you are using dried *porcini*, soak them in 1½ cups of warm water for about 20 minutes. Drain and squeeze out the excess water. Chop coarsely. § Put the garlic and rosemary in a large skillet with the butter and oil and sauté over medium heat for 4-5 minutes. Add the mushrooms and season with salt and pepper. Cover and cook over medium-low heat for about 20-25 minutes, or until the mushrooms are very tender.

§ Cook the pasta in a large pot of salted, boiling water until *al dente*. Drain and place on a heated serving dish. Cover with the sauce and toss vigorously. Serve hot.

■ INGREDIENTS

- 1 pound coarsely chopped fresh porcini mushrooms (or 14 ounces fresh white mushrooms and 2 ounces dried porcini)
- 3 cloves garlic, finely chopped
- sprig of fresh rosemary, finely chopped
- 2 tablespoons butter
- 6 tablespoons extra-virgin olive oil
- salt and freshly ground black pepper
- 14 ounces fresh or dried pasta, or potato gnocchi

Intingolo di noci
Walnut sauce

Walnut sauce is good with fresh pasta and potato gnocchi.

Serves: 4; Preparation: 20 minutes; Cooking: 15 minutes; Level of difficulty: Simple

Roast the pine nuts in the oven at 350° F for 5-10 minutes, or until they are golden in color. Take them out and leave to cool. § Shell the walnuts and combine in a food processor with the pine nuts, garlic, parsley, and oil. Chop finely. Season with salt.

§ Cook the pasta in a large pot of salted, boiling water until *al dente*. Drain thoroughly, transfer to a serving bowl and toss with the sauce. Serve with lots of freshly grated parmesan for sprinkling over each portion.

■ INGREDIENTS

- 1½ pounds walnuts, in their shells
- ¼ cup pine nuts
- 3 cloves garlic
- ¾ cup parsley
- ¾ cup extra virgin olive oil
- salt
- freshly grated parmesan cheese
- 14 ounces fresh pasta or potato gnocchi

Right:
Tagliolini ai funghi porcini

Sugo finto
False "meat" sauce

This light sauce is just as versatile as any meat sauce. Serve it hot with all pasta shapes. For an entirely vegetarian sauce, omit the pancetta and add 1 ounce of dried porcini mushrooms.

Serves: 4; Preparation: 15 minutes; Cooking: 35 minutes; Level of difficulty: Simple

Put the pancetta, parsley, onion, carrots, celery, and garlic in a sauté pan with the oil and butter. Cook over medium-high heat for 5 minutes. Add the tomatoes and season with salt and pepper. Simmer over medium-low heat for about 25 minutes.

§ Cook the pasta in a large pot of salted, boiling water until *al dente*. Drain well and transfer to a heated serving dish. Toss with the sauce and serve hot with lots of freshly grated parmesan on hand to sprinkle over each portion.

■ INGREDIENTS

- ¾ cup diced pancetta
- 1½ cups finely chopped parsley
- 2 medium onions, 3 carrots, 3 stalks celery, 3 cloves garlic, all finely chopped
- 4 tablespoons extra-virgin olive oil
- ¼ cup butter
- 4 large tomatoes, peeled and chopped
- salt and freshly ground black pepper
- freshly grated parmesan cheese
- 14 ounces pasta or gnocchi

Ragù di pesce
Fish sauce

Many different sorts of fish will work in this sauce. Ask your fish vendor for fish that are suitable for making soup. Long, dried shapes, like spaghetti and spaghettini, are the classic choice of pasta. Short, dried pasta shapes, such as penne and maccheroni, are also a good match.

Serves: 4; Preparation: 15 minutes; Cooking: 50 minutes; Level of difficulty: Medium

Place the fish in a pot with abundant water and the rosemary and bring to a boil. Cook for 15 minutes over medium-low heat. Take the fish out, remove the skin and bones, and crumble the cooked meat. Strain the liquid and discard the rosemary leaves. § Sauté the onion and garlic in a large skillet with the oil until light gold in color. Add the fish meat and 3 cups of the broth in which it was cooked. Season with salt and pepper and simmer over low heat for about 30-35 minutes.

§ Cook the pasta in a large pot of salted, boiling water until *al dente*. Drain well and transfer to the skillet with the fish sauce. Add the parsley and toss well. Serve immediately.

■ INGREDIENTS

- 1½-2 pounds assorted fresh fish, such as hake, sea bass, sea bream, and red snapper, gutted
- 3 tablespoons fresh rosemary leaves
- 1 large onion, finely chopped
- 2 cloves garlic, finely chopped
- ⅔ cup extra-virgin olive oil
- salt and freshly ground black pepper
- 2 tablespoons finely chopped parsley
- 14 ounces dried pasta

Right:
Maccheroni al ragù di pesce

BRODO DI CARNE
Meat broth

Homemade meat broth is used as the basis for many soups, to serve tortellini and agnolotti in brodo, and to flavor a number of other pasta dishes. It can be made ahead of time and kept in the refrigerator for up to 3 days. It also freezes well, so make a double quantity and freeze it in small quantities so that you can use as required. Don't worry too much if you don't have one or two of the vegetables, the broth will still be good.

Makes: 1–1½ quarts; Preparation: 15 minutes; Cooking: 3 hours; Level of difficulty: Simple

Put the meat, vegetables, and salt and pepper to taste in a large pot with the water. Cover and bring to a boil over medium heat. Simmer over low heat for 3 hours. Occasionally, skim the scum off the top so that the broth will be light and fresh to taste. § Remove from heat and leave to cool. When the broth is cool, a layer of fat will form on the top. This should be skimmed off.

§ To make *Minestrina in brodo di carne*, allow about 1 cup of broth and about 2 ounces of pasta per person. Put the broth in a saucepan or pot, add the pasta, and simmer until the pasta is *al dente*. Serve hot. Sprinkle each portion with freshly grated parmesan.

VARIATION
– To make chicken broth, replace the beef with chicken.

■ INGREDIENTS

- 2 pounds beef
- 2 pounds meat bones
- 1 carrot
- 1 onion
- 1 stalk celery
- 1 whole clove
- 1 bay leaf
- 1 clove garlic
- 5 sprigs parsley
- 1 leek
- 1 ripe tomato
- 2 quarts water
- salt and freshly ground black pepper
- freshly grated parmesan cheese

BRODO DI PESCE
Fish broth

Fish broth makes a delicious change from meat broth as the basis for minestrine.

Makes: about 2 quarts; Preparation: 15 minutes; Cooking: 1¼ hours; Level of difficulty: Simple

Put the fish and vegetables in a large pot with the water. Bring to a boil. Cover and leave to simmer over low heat for an hour. Season with salt and simmer for 15 more minutes.

§ Serve hot with small, soup pasta shapes following the recipe above for *Minestrina in brodo*, or with *Ravioli di pesce* (see recipe p. 90).

■ INGREDIENTS

- 3 quarts water
- 2½ pounds assorted fresh fish, such as hake, sea bass, sea bream, and red snapper, cleaned and gutted
- 4 stalks celery
- 2 carrots
- 2 medium onions
- 4 cloves garlic
- 4 ripe tomatoes
- 2 tablespoons parsley
- salt

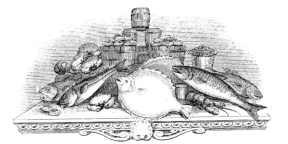

Right:
Minestrina in brodo

DRIED PASTA

By dried pasta we mean store-bought pasta
made from hard-wheat flour and water.
It includes classics such as spaghetti,
penne, fusilli, and maccheroni.

Spaghettini con aglio olio e peperoncino
Spaghettini with garlic, oil and chilies

The sauce is very quick to make and should be used immediately, so begin by cooking the spaghettini in a large pot of salted, boiling water.

Serves: 4; Preparation: 3 minutes; Cooking: 10 minutes; Level of difficulty: Simple

While the pasta is cooking, combine the oil, garlic, and chilies in a small skillet and cook over low heat until the garlic begins to change color. Remove from heat at once, taking care not to burn the garlic because it will give the sauce a bitter flavor. Add the parsley and salt to taste. § Drain the pasta when *al dente* and place in a heated serving dish. Pour the sauce over the pasta and toss vigorously. Serve immediately.

■ INGREDIENTS

- ¾ cup extra-virgin olive oil
- 3 cloves garlic, finely chopped
- ½ teaspoon crushed chilies
- 2 tablespoons finely chopped parsley
- salt
- 14 ounces spaghettini

Wine: a dry white (Trebbiano)

Spaghetti alla carbonara
Spaghetti with eggs and pancetta

La carbonara is a classic Roman sauce. According to some, it was first made during the last days of World War II as American troops advanced up the Italian peninsula bringing supplies of eggs and bacon which they asked the Italians to make into a sauce. Try replacing the pancetta with bacon and decide for yourself about the historical value of this theory.

Serves: 4; Preparation: 5 minutes; Cooking: 15 minutes; Level of difficulty: Simple

Chop the cloves of garlic in half. Combine the oil, garlic, and pancetta in a skillet and sauté over medium heat until the pancetta is golden brown but not crisp. Remove the skillet from the heat and take out the pieces of garlic. § In a mixing bowl lightly beat the eggs, parmesan, pecorino, and salt until smooth. Set aside. § Cook the spaghetti in a large pot of salted, boiling water until *al dente*. Drain and place in a large, heated serving dish. Add the egg mixture and toss. § Return the skillet with the pancetta to high heat for 1 minute. Pour the hot oil and pancetta over the pasta and egg, and toss vigorously. Grind a generous amount of black pepper over the top and serve immediately.

■ INGREDIENTS

- 3 cloves garlic
- 3 tablespoons extra-virgin olive oil
- 1½ cups diced pancetta
- 4 fresh eggs
- 3 tablespoons freshly grated parmesan cheese
- 3 tablespoons freshly grated pecorino cheese
- salt and freshly ground black pepper
- 14 ounces spaghetti

Wine: a light, young red (Vino Novello)

Right:
Spaghetti alla carbonara

Bucatini con capperi e olive

Bucatini with capers and black olives

This simple dish is from Lazio, the region around Rome. If the olives and capers are very salty, you may not need to add any extra salt. Taste the sauce before putting any in.

Serves: 4; Preparation: 10 minutes; Cooking: 15 minutes; Level of difficulty: Simple

Combine the oil, garlic, and parsley in a large sauté pan and cook over medium heat until the garlic starts to change color. Stir the olives and capers into the sauce and cook over low heat for 2-3 minutes. § Cook the bucatini in a large pot of salted, boiling water until *al dente*. Drain and transfer to the sauté pan. Toss with the capers and olives over medium-hot heat for 2 minutes. Place in a heated serving dish and sprinkle with pecorino. Serve hot.

VARIATION
– Replace half the pecorino with parmesan cheese. This will make the sauce slightly "sweeter."

■ INGREDIENTS

• 4 tablespoons extra-virgin olive oil
• 2 cloves garlic, finely chopped
• 3 tablespoons finely chopped parsley
• 1 cup pitted and coarsely chopped black olives
• 3 tablespoons capers
• salt (optional)
• 6 tablespoons freshly grated pecorino cheese
• 14 ounces bucatini

Wine: a dry red (Nebbiolo)

Spaghettini alla puttanesca

Spaghettini with spicy tomato sauce

This sauce is a specialty of the beautiful island of Ischia, off the coast of Naples in southern Italy.

Serves: 4; Preparation: 10 minutes; Cooking: 25-30 minutes; Level of difficulty: Simple

Put the garlic and chilies in a skillet with the oil. Sauté over medium heat until the garlic begins to change color. Add the tomatoes, capers, and olives, and cook for 5 minutes. § Stir the anchovy fillets into the sauce. Season with salt and pepper and simmer over medium heat for 15-20 minutes, or until the oil and tomato begin to separate. § Cook the spaghettini in a large pot of salted, boiling water until *al dente*. Drain and transfer to a heated serving dish. Pour the sauce over the top and toss vigorously. Serve hot.

■ INGREDIENTS

• 2 cloves garlic, finely chopped
• ½ teaspoon crushed chilies
• 4 tablespoons extra-virgin olive oil
• 2¼ cups peeled and chopped fresh or canned tomatoes
• 6 anchovy fillets, lightly crushed with a fork
• 1 cup pitted and coarsely chopped black olives
• 2 tablespoon capers
• salt and freshly ground black pepper
• 14 ounces spaghettini

Wine: a dry white (Vernaccia)

Right: *Bucatini all'amatriciana*

BUCATINI ALL'AMATRICIANA
Bucatini with pancetta and spicy tomato sauce

■ INGREDIENTS

- 1½ cups diced pancetta
- 2 tablespoons extra-virgin olive oil
- 1 onion, finely chopped
- 2 14-ounce cans chopped tomatoes
- ¾ teaspoon crushed chilies
- salt
- 8 tablespoons freshly grated pecorino cheese
- 14 ounces bucatini

Wine: a dry red (Refosco)

Serves: 4; Preparation: 5 minutes; Cooking: 30 minutes; Level of difficulty: Simple

Sauté the pancetta in a skillet with the oil for 2-3 minutes. Add the onion and continue cooking until it becomes transparent. Stir in the tomatoes and chilies. Season with salt and cook over medium-low heat for about 20 minutes, or until the tomatoes have separated from the oil. § Cook the bucatini in a large pot of salted, boiling water until *al dente*. Drain well and transfer to a heated serving bowl. Toss with the sauce and pecorino and serve immediately.

INGREDIENTS

- 10 large ripe tomatoes
- 2 cloves garlic, finely chopped
- 6 tablespoons extra-virgin olive oil
- juice of 1 lemon
- salt and freshly ground black pepper
- 5 ounces fresh mozzarella, diced into ½-inch cubes
- 8 fresh basil leaves, torn
- 14 ounces penne rigate (plain, whole wheat or colored)

Wine: a light, dry white (Pinot grigio)

PENNE CON SALSA DI POMODORO FRESCO
Penne with fresh tomatoes, garlic and mozzarella cheese

This dish is a treat in the summer when ripe, tasty tomatoes are plentiful. It is quick to make and can be varied in a number of ways, according to what you have in the pantry. The sauce is good with many different types of pasta. Try it with spaghetti, fusilli, or cavatappi.

Serves: 4; Preparation: 5 minutes; Cooking: 10 minutes; Level of difficulty: Simple

Peel the tomatoes with a swivel-bladed peeler. Chop them into bite-sized chunks and drain off any extra liquid. Place them in a serving bowl. Add the garlic, 3 tablespoons of the oil, and lemon juice. Season with salt and pepper. § Cook the penne in a large pot of salted, boiling water until *al dente*. Drain well and toss with the remaining oil. § When the pasta is cool, transfer to the bowl with the tomato sauce and toss well. Sprinkle the mozzarella and basil over the top and serve.

VARIATIONS
– Add ⅔ cup black olives.
– Add 2 tablespoons capers.
– Add ½ teaspoon crushed chilies.
– Add 3 tablespoons chopped scallions.

INGREDIENTS

- 1 medium onion, finely chopped
- ¾ cup extra-virgin olive oil
- juice of 3 lemons
- salt and freshly ground black pepper
- 6 tablespoons freshly grated parmesan cheese
- 12 ounces capelli d'angelo

Wine: a dry white (Frascati)

CAPELLI D'ANGELO OLIO E LIMONE
Capelli d'angelo with oil and lemon sauce

Serves: 4; Preparation: 3 minutes; Cooking: 5 minutes; Level of difficulty: Simple

Combine the onion and oil in a large sauté pan. Cook over medium heat until the onion turns golden in color. § Cook the capelli d'angelo in a large pot of salted, boiling water until *al dente*. Drain well and transfer to the pan with the onion. Toss the pasta briefly with the onion over medium heat and transfer to a large, heated serving dish. Add the lemon juice, salt, pepper, and parmesan. Toss well and serve immediately.

Left:
Capelli d'angelo olio e limoni

VARIATION
– For a creamier sauce, toss a raw egg yolk together with the lemon juice and parmesan.

PENNE ALL'ARRABBIATA
Penne with "angry" tomato sauce

Serves: 4; Preparation: 15 minutes; Cooking: 30 minutes; Level of difficulty: Simple

Put the pancetta, garlic, celery, and onion in a large sauté pan with the oil and cook until lightly browned. Add the tomatoes, mint, basil, parsley, and chilies. Season with salt and pepper. Simmer over medium-low heat for about 20 minutes or until the tomatoes and oil begin to separate. § Cook the penne in a large pot of salted, boiling water until *al dente*. Drain and toss with the sauce in the pan over high heat for 2-3 minutes. Transfer to a heated serving dish and serve hot.

VARIATIONS
- Double the amount of chilies for a really firey dish.
- Add 4 tablespoons grated pecorino cheese just before serving.

■ INGREDIENTS

- ¾ cup diced pancetta
- 4 cloves garlic, 1 celery stalk, 1 medium onion, all finely chopped
- ⅓ cup extra-virgin olive oil
- 3 cups peeled and chopped ripe tomatoes
- 6 fresh mint leaves, torn
- 6 fresh basil leaves, torn
- 3 tablespoons finely chopped parsley
- ½ teaspoon crushed chilies
- salt and freshly ground black pepper
- 14 ounces penne rigate

*Wine: a dry red
(Montepulciano d'Abruzzo)*

PENNE CON I CARCIOFI
Penne with artichokes

Serves: 4; Preparation: 30 minutes; Cooking: 30 minutes; Level of difficulty: Simple

Wash the artichokes and remove all but the pale inner leaves by pulling the outer ones down and snapping them off. Cut off the stalk and the top third of the remaining leaves. Remove any tough pieces of leaves at the base with a sharp knife. Cut the artichokes in half lengthwise and scrape the fuzzy choke away with the knife. Cut each artichoke half into thin slices lengthwise and place in a bowl of cold water with the lemon juice. Soak for 20 minutes. Remove and pat dry with paper towels. § Put the oil and garlic in a large sauté pan and cook until the garlic begins to change color. Add the artichokes and cook over medium-low heat for about 25 minutes, or until the artichokes are very tender. Add water if all the oil has been absorbed. Season with salt and pepper. § Cook the penne in a large pot of salted, boiling water until *al dente*. Drain well and toss with the artichoke sauce over high heat for 2-3 minutes. Sprinkle with the parsley and pecorino. Serve hot.

■ INGREDIENTS

- 8 artichokes
- juice of 1 lemon
- ½ cup extra-virgin olive oil
- 3 cloves garlic, finely chopped
- salt and freshly ground black pepper
- 4 tablespoons finely chopped parsley
- 5 tablespoons freshly grated pecorino cheese
- 14 ounces penne lisce or rigate

*Wine: a dry white
(Orvieto)*

Right:
Penne con i carciofi

- ¾ cup milk
- 1 cup fresh ricotta cheese
- 1 tablespoon sugar
- 1 teaspoon cinnamon
- salt
- white pepper
- 14 ounces penne lisce or rigate

Wine: a light, dry white (Verdicchio)

PENNE CON RICOTTA
Penne with ricotta cheese

This is a classic southern Italian recipe. It is very simple and everything depends on the quality and freshness of the ricotta. Buy it loose from a specialty cheese shop or a good Italian deli. This sauce is also good with homemade fettuccine (see recipe p. 120-122).

Serves: 4; Preparation: 5 minutes; Cooking: 10 minutes; Level of difficulty: Simple

Warm the milk and place in a bowl with the ricotta, sugar, cinnamon, and a dash of salt and white pepper. Mix with a fork to form a smooth, creamy sauce. § Cook the penne in a large pot of salted, boiling water until *al dente*. Drain well and place in a heated serving bowl. Toss with the sauce and serve.

FESTONATI CON SALSICCE E BROCCOLI
Festonati with Italian sausages and broccoli

Serves: 4; Preparation: 10 minutes; Cooking: 30 minutes; Level of difficulty: Simple

Divide the broccoli into florets of about ¾ inch in diameter. Cut the stems into ½-inch cubes. Plunge the florets and stems into a large pot of salted, boiling water and cook for about 5 minutes, or until tender-crunchy. Drain well and set aside. § Place the oil in a large sauté pan with the garlic and parsley over medium heat. When the garlic begins to change color, add the sausages and tomato paste. Cook over medium heat for 5 minutes. Add the broccoli, season with salt and pepper and cook for 10-15 minutes. § Cook the festonati in a large pot of salted, boiling water until *al dente*. Drain and toss with the sauce. Sprinkle with pecorino and serve hot.

VARIATION
– Add a thinly sliced leek to the garlic and parsley. It will take 3-4 minutes extra to cook.

■ INGREDIENTS

• 12 ounces broccoli
• 3 tablespoons extra-virgin olive oil
• 3 cloves garlic, finely chopped
• 2 tablespoons finely chopped parsley
• 9 ounces Italian pork sausages, skinned and crumbled
• 2 tablespoons tomato paste
• salt and freshly ground black pepper
• 5 tablespoons freshly grated pecorino cheese
• 14 ounces festonati

Wine: a young, dry red (Vino Novello)

RIGATONI CON GLI ZUCCHINI
Rigatoni with zucchini

Serves: 4; Preparation: 10 minutes; Cooking: 25 minutes; Level of difficulty: Simple

Heat the butter and oil together in a skillet. Cut the clove of garlic in half, add to the skillet, and sauté until it starts to change color. Remove the garlic pieces and add the zucchini. Sauté over a high heat until the zucchini begin to turn golden brown. § Turn the heat down, cover the pan with a lid, and simmer until the zucchini are tender. Season with salt and pepper. § Cook the rigatoni in a large pot of salted, boiling water until *al dente*. Drain and transfer to a heated serving dish. Add the zucchini, parsley, and parmesan, and toss well. Serve hot.

VARIATIONS
– Add ½ teaspoon crushed chilies for a spicy dish.
– If you prefer crunchy vegetables, add the zucchini to the pasta as soon as they are golden brown, without simmering until tender.

■ INGREDIENTS

• 3 tablespoons butter
• 3 tablespoons extra-virgin olive oil
• 2 cloves garlic
• 6 zucchini, sliced into thin wheels
• salt and freshly ground black pepper
• 3 tablespoons finely chopped parsley
• 6 tablespoons freshly grated parmesan cheese
• 14 ounces rigatoni

Wine: a dry white (Orvieto Classico)

Right:
Festonati con salsicce e broccoli

Spaghetti allo scoglio
Spaghetti with shellfish sauce

Serves: 4: Preparation: 15 minutes; Cooking: 35 minutes; Level of difficulty: Simple

Scrub the mussels and clams and soak them in cold water for 5 minutes. § Put half the garlic and 2 tablespoons of the oil in a skillet. Sauté over medium heat until the garlic begins to change color. Add the tomatoes, basil, half the parsley, and the vinegar. Season with salt and pepper and leave to simmer for about 20 minutes. § Put the remaining oil, garlic, parsley, and slices of lemon in a large sauté pan. Cook over medium heat until the garlic begins to change color. Add the mussels and clams and turn up the heat. When all the shellfish are open, add them (with their liquid) to the pan with the tomato sauce. Simmer for about 10 minutes, or until the sauce has reduced. § Cook the spaghetti in a large pot of salted, boiling water until *al dente*. Drain and transfer to a heated serving dish. Pour the sauce over the top and toss well. Serve immediately.

VARIATIONS
- Add ½ teaspoon crushed chilies to the garlic and oil.
- Add 2 crushed bay leaves to the oil and lemon sauce.

■ INGREDIENTS

- 24 mussels in shell
- 36 clams in shell
- 4 cloves garlic, finely chopped
- 6 tablespoons extra-virgin olive oil
- 3 cups peeled and chopped ripe tomatoes
- 9 fresh basil leaves, torn
- 8 tablespoons finely chopped parsley
- 1½ teaspoons vinegar
- salt and freshly ground black pepper
- 4 slices of lemon
- 14 ounces spaghetti

Wine: a light, dry white (Vermentino)

Spaghetti alle vongole
Spaghetti with clams

Serves: 4; Preparation: 10 minutes; Cooking: 30 minutes; Level of difficulty: Simple

Scrub the clams thoroughly and soak in cold water for 5 minutes. § Put 2 tablespoons of the oil in a large sauté pan and warm over medium heat. Add the clams and white wine, and cook until all the clams are open. Remove the clams, discarding any that have not opened, and set aside. Put the remaining liquid in a bowl and set aside. § Combine the remaining oil and garlic in the same pan and cook until the garlic begins to change color. Add the tomatoes and cook over medium heat for about 5 minutes. Pour in the clam liquid. Season with salt and pepper. Cook for 15 more minutes, or until the sauce becomes thick. Add the clams and parsley, and continue cooking for 2-3 minutes. § Cook the spaghetti in a large pot of salted, boiling water until *al dente*. Drain and transfer to the sauté pan with the sauce. Toss for 1-2 minutes over medium-hot heat. Serve immediately.

■ INGREDIENTS

- 50 clams in shell
- 6 tablespoons extra-virgin olive oil
- 6 tablespoons dry white wine
- 3 cloves garlic, finely chopped
- 6 ripe tomatoes, peeled and chopped
- salt and freshly ground black pepper
- 2 tablespoons finely chopped parsley
- 14 ounces spaghetti

Wine: a dry white (Tocai)

Right:
Spaghetti alle vongole

INGREDIENTS

- ⅓ cup butter
- ¾ cup vodka
- juice of 1½ lemons
- 3 ounces smoked salmon
- 3 teaspoons caviar
- 3 tablespoons fresh cream
- salt and freshly ground black pepper
- 14 ounces farfalle

Wine: a dry white

(Soave)

Farfalle al salmone e vodka
Farfalle with smoked salmon and vodka sauce

Serves: 4; Preparation: 5 minutes; Cooking: 15 minutes; Level of difficulty: Simple

Put the butter, vodka, and lemon juice in a heavy-bottomed pan. Cook over low heat until the vodka has evaporated. Crumble the smoked salmon with a fork. Add the salmon and caviar to the pan. Cook over medium-low heat for 2-3 minutes. Add the cream and salt and pepper to taste. Remove from heat. § Cook the farfalle in a large pot of salted, boiling water until *al dente*. Drain well and transfer to the pan. Toss over medium heat and serve immediately.

Spaghetti con le seppie
Spaghetti with cuttlefish

Serves 4; Preparation: 20 minutes; Cooking: about 1 hour; Level of difficulty: Medium

Rinse the cuttlefish thoroughly in cold water. To clean, cut each cuttlefish lengthwise and remove the internal bone and the stomach. Take care not to break the internal ink sac. Set the sacs aside. Cut the cuttlefish crosswise into thin half circles. § Combine the onion and garlic in a large sauté pan with the oil and cook over medium heat until they begin to change color. Add the cuttlefish and tomato pulp. Season with salt and pepper. Turn the heat down low, cover, and simmer for about 45 minutes, or until the cuttlefish are tender. § Add the ink and stir over medium heat for 2-3 minutes. § Cook the spaghetti in a large pot of salted, boiling water until *al dente*. Drain well and transfer to a heated serving dish. Toss vigorously with the sauce and serve hot.

■ INGREDIENTS

- 8 cuttlefish
- 1 large onion
- 2 cloves garlic, finely chopped
- ½ cup extra-virgin olive oil
- 1 cup canned tomato pulp
- salt and freshly ground black pepper
- 14 ounces spaghetti

Wine: a dry white (Pinot Grigio)

Linguine con le fave
Linguine with fava beans and fresh rosemary

If fresh fava beans are out of season, use 1-1¼ pounds of frozen ones. This sauce is also good with many short pastas, such as conchiglie, lumaconi, or rigatoni.

Serves: 4; Preparation: 15 minutes; Cooking: about 30 minutes; Level of difficulty: Simple

Pod the beans and set aside in a bowl of cold water. § Cut the clove of garlic in two and combine with the rosemary, half the butter, and the oil in a skillet. Sauté over medium heat until the garlic begins to change color. Remove the garlic and rosemary, making sure that none of the leaves remain in the sauce. Lower heat to medium, add the onion, and sauté until transparent. § Drain the fava beans and add with the broth to the skillet. Season with salt and pepper. Continue to cook over medium-low heat for about 20 minutes or until the beans are tender, stirring from time to time. § Cook the linguine in a large pot of salted, boiling water until *al dente*. Drain and place in a heated serving dish. Pour the sauce over the pasta and toss with the parmesan and the remaining butter until well mixed. Serve hot.

■ INGREDIENTS

- 3 pounds fava beans in their pods
- 2 cloves garlic
- 3 sprigs fresh rosemary
- ⅓ cup butter
- 3 tablespoons extra-virgin olive oil
- 1 large onion, finely chopped
- 1½ cups meat broth (see recipe p. 34)
- salt and freshly ground black pepper
- 6 tablespoons freshly grated parmesan cheese
- 14 ounces linguine

Wine: a light, dry white (Verdicchio)

Right:
Linguine con le fave

■ INGREDIENTS

- ½ cup extra-virgin olive oil
- 2½ cups peeled and chopped ripe tomatoes
- 2 teaspoons oregano
- salt and freshly ground black pepper
- 6 ounces diced fresh mozzarella cheese
- 5 tablespoons freshly grated pecorino cheese
- 14 ounces fusilli

Wine: a dry white (Greco di Tufo)

Fusilli alla Vesuviana
Fusilli with tomato and mozzarella cheese

This dish comes from Campania, the region of which Naples is the capital city. The volcano Vesuvius towers above the Bay of Naples and has given its name to this dish invented in its shadows.

Serves: 4; Preparation: 10 minutes; Cooking: 20 minutes; Level of difficulty: Simple

Place the oil in a skillet over medium heat. Add the tomatoes, oregano, salt and pepper, and cook for about 15 minutes, stirring from time to time. When the tomatoes begin to separate from the oil, remove from heat. § Cook the fusilli in a large pot of salted, boiling water until *al dente*. Drain well and place in a heated serving dish. Add the mozzarella and pecorino and toss vigorously. Serve immediately.

■ INGREDIENTS

- ½ cup extra-virgin olive oil
- 1 medium green, 1 medium yellow, and 1 medium red bell pepper
- 1 large onion, finely chopped
- 2 cloves garlic, finely chopped
- 1¼ cups peeled and chopped ripe tomatoes
- 9 basil leaves, torn
- 3 tablespoons boiling water
- salt and freshly ground black pepper
- 3 tablespoons vinegar
- 6 anchovy fillets
- 14 ounces maccheroni

Wine: a dry red (Chianti Classico)

Maccheroni con i Peperoni
Maccheroni with bell peppers

Serves: 4; Preparation: 10 minutes; Cooking: 40 minutes; Level of difficulty: Simple

Cut the bell peppers in half lengthwise. Remove stalks, seeds and membrane, and cut crosswise into strips about ⅛-¼ inch in width. § Combine oil, bell peppers, onion, and garlic in a large skillet and sauté until the garlic turns golden brown. Add the tomatoes, basil, and boiling water. Season with salt and pepper. Simmer over medium heat for 20-25 minutes or until the bell peppers are tender, stirring from time to time. § Stir in the vinegar and anchovies, and cook over high heat for 2-3 minutes until the vinegar evaporates. Remove from heat. § Cook the maccheroni in a large pot of salted, boiling water until *al dente*. Drain well and transfer to a heated serving dish. Pour the sauce over the top and toss until well mixed. Serve hot.

VARIATION
— For a more filling, cold-weather dish, place the cooked pasta in a baking dish, pour the sauce over the top and mix well. Spread 7 ounces thinly sliced mozzarella cheese on top and bake in preheated oven at 350° F for 10 minutes or until the mozzarella turns golden brown.

Left:
Fusilli alla vesuviana

Spaghettini al tonno
Spaghettini with tuna and tomato sauce

Ideally you should use caciocavallo cheese, but if this is not available, use a tasty pecorino instead. Don't use parmesan in this recipe.

Serves: 4: Preparation: 15 minutes; Cooking: 35 minutes; Level of difficulty: Simple

Put the oil, garlic, onion, and anchovy to cook in a large sauté pan over a medium-high heat for 3-4 minutes. Add the tomatoes and simmer over medium-low heat for 25 minutes, stirring from time to time. § Stir in the tuna, oregano, and black pepper. Taste the sauce and, if necessary, add salt. Simmer over medium heat for another 5 minutes. § Cook the spaghettini in a large pot of salted, boiling water until *al dente*. Drain well and transfer to a heated serving dish. Toss with the sauce and cheese. Serve hot.

Bucatoni con le cipolle
Bucatoni with onion sauce

Serves: 4; Preparation: 5 minutes; Cooking: 50 minutes; Level of difficulty: Simple

Put the onions in a sauté pan with the butter and oil. Sauté over medium heat until they begin to change color. Add salt and pepper to taste. § Turn the heat down to low, cover, and simmer for about 40 minutes, or until the onions are very soft. § Uncover and add the wine. Turn the heat up to medium and stir while the wine evaporates. Remove from heat. § Break the thick bucatoni noodles in half and cook in a large pot of salted, boiling water until they are *al dente*. Drain well and transfer to a heated serving dish. Pour the onion sauce over the top. Add the parsley and parmesan, and toss vigorously until the sauce and pasta are well mixed. Serve hot.

■ INGREDIENTS

- 7 tablespoons extra-virgin olive oil
- 3 cloves garlic, finely chopped
- 2 medium onions, finely chopped
- 2 anchovy fillets
- 2¼ cups peeled and chopped fresh or canned tomatoes
- 2 4-ounce cans tuna fish
- 1 teaspoon dried oregano
- ¾ cup freshly grated caciocavallo (or pecorino) cheese
- salt and freshly ground black pepper
- 14 ounces spaghettini

Wine: a light, dry white (Galestro)

■ INGREDIENTS

- 5 large onions, sliced in thin rings
- ⅓ cup butter
- 3 tablespoons extra-virgin olive oil
- salt and freshly ground black pepper
- ¾ cup dry white wine
- 3 tablespoons finely chopped parsley
- 8 tablespoons freshly grated parmesan cheese
- 14 ounces bucatoni

Wine: a dry white (Orvieto)

Right:
Farfalle con piselli e prosciutto

- 1¼ cups fresh or frozen peas
- ⅓ cup butter
- 6 ounces ham, diced into ¼-inch cubes
- 3 tablespoons fresh cream
- 2 tablespoons finely chopped parsley
- salt and freshly ground black pepper
- 4 tablespoons freshly grated parmesan cheese
- 14 ounces farfalle

FARFALLE CON PISELLI E PROSCIUTTO
Farfalle with peas and ham

Serves: 4; Preparation: 5 minutes; Cooking: 20 minutes; Level of difficulty: Simple

Boil the peas in salted water until half cooked. § Combine the peas, butter, and ham in a large skillet. Cook over medium-low heat for 10 minutes. Stir in 1 tablespoon of the cream and continue cooking until the sauce becomes thick. Add the parsley, and salt and pepper to taste. § Cook the farfalle in a large pot of salted, boiling water until *al dente*. Drain well and transfer to the skillet with the sauce. Add the remaining cream and parmesan. Toss well and serve hot.

Lumaconi all'ortolana
Lumaconi with vegetables

Serves: 4-6; Preparation: 10 minutes; Cooking: 35 minutes; Level of difficulty: Simple

Chop the onion coarsely. Peel the eggplant and dice it and the zucchini into bite-sized cubes. Remove the stalks and cores from the peppers and chop into ½-inch square pieces. Put the onion in a large sauté pan with the oil and cook over medium heat until it becomes transparent. Add the eggplant, bell peppers and zucchini. Sauté the vegetables for 7-8 minutes. Add the tomatoes, crushed chilies, and salt to taste. Cook for 20 minutes. § Cook the lumaconi in a large pot of salted, boiling water until *al dente*. Drain and add to the sauté pan with the vegetables. Toss over high heat for 2-3 minutes until well mixed. Add the basil and parmesan. Transfer to a heated serving dish and serve hot.

Conchiglie al cavolfiore
Conchiglie with cauliflower, garlic and chilies

Serves: 4-6; Preparation: 5 minutes; Cooking: 25 minutes; Level of difficulty: Simple

Divide the cauliflower into bite-sized florets and dice the stalk into ½-inch cubes. Cook in boiling water until half cooked (about 7 minutes). Drain and set aside. § Combine the oil, butter, and onion in a large skillet and sauté until the onion is transparent. Add the garlic and crushed chilies and sauté until garlic begins to change color. Add the cauliflower pieces and cook over medium-low heat for 8-10 more minutes, or until the cauliflower is tender. Season with salt and pepper. § Cook the conchiglie in a large pot of salted, boiling water until *al dente*. Drain well and transfer to the skillet. Toss the pasta and sauce together over medium heat for 2-3 minutes. Serve hot.

VARIATIONS
- Replace the cauliflower with green broccoli.
- Add 6 ripe peeled tomatoes to the skillet with the cauliflower pieces.

■ INGREDIENTS

- 1 large onion
- 1 large eggplant
- 2 large zucchini
- 1 small green, 1 small yellow, and 1 small red bell pepper
- ⅓ cup extra-virgin olive oil
- 2 14-ounce cans chopped tomatoes
- ½ teaspoon crushed chilies
- salt
- 8 basil leaves, torn
- 4 tablespoons freshly grated parmesan cheese
- 14 ounces lumaconi

Wine: a dry white (Bianco San Severo)

■ INGREDIENTS

- 1 large cauliflower
- 4 tablespoons extra-virgin olive oil
- 3 tablespoons butter
- 1 medium onion
- 4 cloves garlic, finely chopped
- ¾ teaspoon crushed chilies
- salt and freshly ground black pepper
- 14 ounces conchiglie

Wine: a light, dry white (Cortese)

Right: *Conchiglie al cavolfiore* and *Lumaconi all'ortolana*

MALLOREDDUS
Malloreddus with Italian sausages and pecorino cheese

Malloreddus ("little bulls"), or gnocchi sardi *as they are also known, are a specialty of the island of Sardinia. They are quite unlike the other dried pasta in this section, being made of bran flour and saffron. Malloreddus can be made fresh at home, but it is a difficult and time-consuming task and good commercial varieties are now available in specialty stores.*

Serves: 4; Preparation: 5 minutes; Cooking: 30 minutes; Level of difficulty: Simple

Combine the oil, sausages, onion, garlic, and basil in a skillet and sauté over medium heat until the onion turns golden brown. Add the tomatoes and salt and pepper to taste. Simmer for 15-20 minutes or until the sauce becomes thick. § Cook the malloreddus in a large pot of salted, boiling water until *al dente*. Drain well and transfer to a heated serving dish. Add the sauce and pecorino, and toss. Serve hot with lots of pecorino or parmesan on hand to sprinkle over each portion.

SPAGHETTI ALLA NORMA
Spaghetti with fried eggplant

Pasta alla Norma *is a classic Sicilian dish. Debate rages about the origins of the name. Some say that it is named after Bellini's famous opera. Others maintain that it simply means* la norma, *or something that happens often. It may also derive from the Catanese dialect, in which* norma *means "the very best."*

Serves: 4; Preparation: 1½ hours; Cooking: 40 minutes; Level of difficulty: Simple

Cut the eggplants into ¼-inch thick slices, sprinkle with salt and place on a slanted cutting board, so that the bitter liquid they produce can run off. This will take about an hour. § Put the olive oil and garlic in a skillet over medium heat and cook until the garlic turns gold. Add the tomatoes, basil, and salt and pepper to taste. Cook over medium-low heat for about 20 minutes, or until the oil and tomatoes begin to separate. § Run the eggplant under cold water and pat dry with paper towels. Put about 1¼-inches of vegetable oil in a large skillet. When the oil is very hot, add as many slices of eggplant as will fit without overlapping. Fry to golden brown on both sides and place on paper towels. When all the eggplant is fried, chop into large squares. § Cook the spaghetti in a large pot of salted, boiling water until *al dente*. Drain well and transfer to a heated serving dish. Toss with the tomato sauce and fried eggplant. Sprinkle with the pecorino and serve hot.

■ INGREDIENTS

- 3 tablespoons extra-virgin olive oil
- 9 ounces Italian pork sausages, skinned and crumbled
- 1 large onion, finely chopped
- 3 cloves garlic, finely chopped
- 8 basil leaves, torn
- 3½ cups fresh peeled and chopped tomatoes
- salt and freshly ground black pepper
- 6 tablespoons freshly grated pecorino cheese
- 14 ounces malloreddus

Wine: a dry red, preferably Sardinian, such as a Cannonau (be warned though, Sardinian wines are notoriously strong and some Cannonaus, particularly when aged, can reach 15-17 percent alcohol content).

■ INGREDIENTS

- 3 large eggplants
- salt and freshly ground black pepper
- 3 tablespoons extra-virgin olive oil
- 3 cloves garlic, finely chopped
- 3 cups peeled and chopped tomatoes
- 2 tablespoons basil, torn
- vegetable oil for frying
- ¾ cup freshly grated pecorino cheese
- 14 ounces spaghetti

Wine: rosé (Cirò Superiore)

Right:
Malloreddus

Bavette con fagiolini e pesto
Bavette with green beans, potatoes and pesto

If you order pasta with pesto sauce in its hometown of Genoa, it will almost certainly be served with potatoes and green beans.

Serves: 4; Preparation: 15 minutes; Cooking: 25 minutes; Level of difficulty: Simple

Cook the vegetables in a large pot of salted, boiling water until tender. Take them out with a slotted spoon and use the same water to cook the pasta. § While the pasta is cooking, prepare the pesto. Add 2 tablespoons of boiling water from the pasta pot to make the pesto slightly more liquid. § When the pasta is cooked *al dente*, drain and transfer to a heated serving dish. Toss with the pesto, butter, and vegetables. Sprinkle with the pecorino and parmesan, and serve hot.

■ INGREDIENTS

- 3 cups green beans, fresh or frozen, cut into 1¼-inch lengths
- 3 medium new potatoes, peeled and diced in ½-inch cubes
- 1½ quantities of pesto (see recipe p. 28)
- 3 tablespoons butter
- 2 tablespoons freshly grated pecorino cheese
- 2 tablespoons freshly grated parmesan cheese
- 14 ounces bavette

Wine: a dry white (Vermentino)

Orecchiette con le bietole
Orecchiette with chard

Orecchiette ("little ears") come from Puglia in southern Italy. Like malloreddus, they can also be made at home using bran flour but it is a laborious task. It is much easier to buy them readymade at specialty stores. They are good with the vegetable sauces suggested below, but can also be served with meat sauce (see p. 26), tomato sauces (see p. 22), or garlic, oil and chili sauce (see p. 38).

Serves: 4; Preparation: 10 minutes; Cooking: 15 minutes; Level of difficulty: Simple

Cook the chard in a pot of salted boiling water (3-4 minutes for frozen, 8-10 minutes for fresh). Drain well and squeeze out any extra moisture. Chop finely. § Combine the garlic and crumbled anchovy fillet in a large sauté pan with the oil. Sauté until the garlic turns gold in color. Add the chard. Season with salt and pepper. § Cook the orecchiette in a large pot of salted, boiling water until *al dente*. Drain well and transfer to the sauté pan with the sauce. Toss for 1-2 minutes over medium-high heat. Serve immediately with lots of freshly grated pecorino for sprinkling on each portion.

■ INGREDIENTS

- 1 pound fresh or 12 ounces frozen chard
- 3 cloves garlic, finely chopped
- 8 tablespoons extra-virgin olive oil
- 2 anchovy fillets, crumbled
- salt and freshly ground black pepper
- freshly grated pecorino
- 14 ounces orecchiette

Wine: a dry red (Barolo)

Right:
Orecchiette con le bietole

VARIATIONS
– If you like hot dishes this one works very well with ½ teaspoon crushed chilies.
– For slightly different but equally delicious dishes, replace the chard with the same quantity of florets and diced stalks of green broccoli or cauliflower, or shredded savoy cabbage.

INGREDIENTS

- 1½ pounds fresh asparagus
- 3 tablespoons butter
- 8 ounces ham, cut into thin strips
- 1 cup fresh cream
- 8 tablespoons freshly grated parmesan cheese
- salt and freshly ground black pepper
- 14 ounces penne

Wine: a dry white (Soave)

PENNE CON GLI ASPARAGI
Penne with asparagus

Serves: 4; Preparation: 10 minutes; Cooking: 15 minutes; Level of difficulty: Simple

Cook the asparagus in a pot of salted, boiling water until the tips are tender. Drain and remove the hard parts from each stalk. § Melt the butter in a saucepan with the ham. Cook for 2-3 minutes. Add the asparagus tips and the cream, and stir gently over medium heat for 3-4 minutes, or until the cream thickens. Season with salt and pepper. § Cook the penne in a large pot of salted, boiling water until *al dente*. Drain and place in a heated serving dish. Add the sauce and toss well. Sprinkle with the parmesan and serve hot.

Fusilli lunghi ai porri
Fusilli lunghi with leeks

Serves: 4; Preparation: 10 minutes; Cooking: 40 minutes; Level of difficulty: Simple

Prepare the leeks by discarding two layers of outer leaves and cutting off almost all the top green part. Slice in thin wheels. Set aside. § Combine butter, oil, onion, and garlic in a skillet and sauté over medium heat until the onion turns golden in color. Add the pancetta and stir so that it browns on all sides. Add the leeks and boiling water (from the pasta pot) and simmer over low heat until the leeks are very tender. Season with salt and pepper. Add the egg yolk and sugar, and stir vigorously. Remove from heat. § Cook the fusilli in a large pot of salted, boiling water until *al dente*. Drain well and transfer to a heated serving dish. Toss with the sauce, sprinkle with pecorino, and serve hot.

■ **INGREDIENTS**

- 10 leeks
- 2 tablespoons butter
- 6 tablespoons extra-virgin olive oil
- 1 large onion, finely chopped
- 2 cloves garlic, finely chopped
- ¾ cup diced pancetta
- 1¼ cups boiling water
- salt and freshly ground black pepper
- 2 egg yolks
- dash of sugar
- 4 tablespoons freshly grated pecorino cheese
- 14 ounces fusilli lunghi

Wine: a light, dry red (Lambrusco)

Spaghetti alla carrettiera
Spaghetti with onion, garlic and bread crumbs

This is a classic Roman recipe. It is said to have been the favorite dish of the carrettieri *(cart-drivers) who transported the Castelli Romani wine from the Alban Hills into Rome. There are many variations on the basic recipe given here. We have suggested the common tomato one below.*

Serves: 4; Preparation: 10 minutes; Cooking: 15 minutes; Level of difficulty: Simple

Place the onion, garlic and parsley in a sauté pan with the oil, oregano, salt and pepper to taste and sauté over medium heat until the onion and garlic turn golden in color. Remove from heat. § Toast the bread crumbs in the oven and mix with a few drops of oil. § Cook the spaghetti in a large pot of salted, boiling water until *al dente*. Drain well and transfer to a heated serving dish. Toss with the sauce and bread crumbs, and serve hot.

■ **INGREDIENTS**

- 1 large onion, finely chopped
- 2 cloves garlic, finely chopped
- 2 tablespoons finely chopped parsley
- 6 tablespoons extra-virgin olive oil
- 1 teaspoon oregano
- salt and freshly ground black pepper
- 3 tablespoons bread crumbs
- 14 ounces spaghetti

Wine: a dry white (Velletri)

Right:
Fusilli lunghi ai porri

VARIATION
- Add 6 medium peeled tomatoes and ¾ teaspoon crushed chilies to the onion and garlic mixture after it has changed color. Cook over medium heat for 10-15 minutes or until the tomatoes have reduced.

Fresh Pasta

Fresh pasta is made of egg and soft-wheat flour. It includes old favorites like tagliatelle, fettuccine, and tagliolini. With a little practise you can learn to make delicious fresh pasta at home.

TAGLIOLINI AL MASCARPONE
Tagliolini with mascarpone cheese sauce

The success of this simple sauce lies in the speed and accuracy with which the tagliolini are tossed with the mascarpone and egg. When the pasta comes in contact with the egg, it should still be hot enough to harden the yolk a little so that the whole sauce becomes creamy.

Serves: 4; Preparation: 5 minutes; Cooking: 5 minutes; Level of difficulty: Simple

Warm the mascarpone in a saucepan. Remove from heat and stir in the egg yolk. Season with salt. § Cook the tagliolini in a large pot of salted, boiling water until *al dente*. Drain well and toss with the mascarpone and egg sauce. Sprinkle with the parmesan and freshly ground black pepper. Serve hot.

> VARIATION
> – Add ½ teaspoon freshly ground nutmeg to the mascarpone and egg.

■ INGREDIENTS

- 1 cup fresh mascarpone cheese
- 2 egg yolks
- salt and freshly ground black pepper
- 8 tablespoons freshly grated parmesan cheese
- 14 ounces store-bought tagliolini

Wine: a light, dry white (Verdicchio di Matelica)

TAGLIATELLE ALLE VONGOLE CON PANNA
Tagliatelle with clams and cream

Serves: 4; Preparation: 10 minutes + time needed to make the pasta; Cooking: 15 minutes; Level of difficulty: Simple

Put the clams in a large sauté pan, cover, and place over high heat until they are all open. Remove from the pan and set aside with their juice. § Sauté the garlic in the same pan over medium heat with the oil, chilies, and bay leaves. When the garlic begins to change color, add the clams and their juice, the cream, tomatoes, and salt to taste. Simmer over medium heat for 5-10 minutes, or until the sauce has reduced sufficiently. § Cook the tagliatelle in a large pot of salted, boiling water until *al dente*. Drain well and transfer to the sauté pan with the clams. Toss quickly over medium-high heat and serve immediately.

■ INGREDIENTS

- 1½ quarts clams in shell
- 2 cloves garlic, finely chopped
- 3 tablespoons extra-virgin olive oil
- ½ teaspoon crushed chilies
- 3 bay leaves
- ¾ cup fresh cream
- 3 large tomatoes, peeled and chopped
- salt
- 14 ounces store-bought or homemade tagliatelle (see recipe pp. 120-122)

Wine: a dry white (Pinot bianco)

Right:
Tagliolini al mascarpone

Pappardelle sulla lepre
Pappardelle with wild hare sauce

*This is a classic Tuscan dish. Traditionally the recipe calls
for wild hare, but if this is hard to find
use the same amount of rabbit in its place.*

*Serves: 4; Preparation: 20 minutes + time needed to make the pasta; Cooking: 2½ hours; Level of
difficulty: Medium*

Sauté the parsley, rosemary, onion, carrot, and celery with the oil in a
heavy-bottomed pan over medium heat. When the onion and garlic
begin to change color, add the hare meat and cook for 15-20 minutes
or until the meat is well browned, stirring frequently. Add the wine
and stir until it has evaporated. § Add the boiling water, milk, and
tomato paste. Season with salt and pepper. Simmer over low heat for
about 1½ hours. § Add the hare liver and, if necessary, more water.
Cook for 30 more minutes or until the hare is very tender. § Cook the
pappardelle in a large pot of salted, boiling water until *al dente*. Drain
well and place in a heated serving dish. Toss with the sauce and
sprinkle with parmesan. Serve hot.

■ INGREDIENTS

- 3 tablespoons parsley, 1½ tablespoons fresh rosemary, 1 large onion, 1 large carrot, 1 stalk celery, all finely chopped
- ¾ cup extra-virgin olive oil
- 1¼ pounds boneless wild hare meat, with liver, coarsely chopped
- 3 cups red wine
- 4 cups boiling water
- ½ cup milk
- 2 tablespoons tomato paste
- salt and freshly ground black pepper
- 4 tablespoons freshly grated parmesan cheese
- 14 ounces store-bought or homemade pappardelle (see recipe pp. 120-122)

*Wine: a dry red
(Chianti dei Colli Aretini)*

Tagliatelle al prosciutto
Tagliatelle with prosciutto

*Serves: 4; Preparation: 5 minutes + time needed to make the pasta; Cooking: 10-12 minutes; Level
of difficulty: Simple*

Sauté the onion and fat from the prosciutto with the butter in a skillet
until the onion begins to change color. Add the prosciutto and sauté for
2-3 minutes. Add the wine, and salt and pepper to taste. Simmer until the
wine evaporates. § Cook the tagliatelle in a large pot of salted boiling water
until *al dente*. Drain well and place in a heated serving dish. Pour the sauce
over the top and toss vigorously. Sprinkle with parmesan and serve hot.

■ INGREDIENTS

- 1 medium onion, finely chopped
- 8 ounces prosciutto, diced in ½-inch cubes
- ⅓ cup butter
- ¾ cup dry white wine
- salt and freshly ground black pepper
- 4 tablespoons freshly grated parmesan cheese
- 14 ounces store-bought or homemade tagliatelle (see recipe pp. 120-122)

*Wine: a rosé
(Rosato di Carmignano)*

Right:
Pappardelle sulla lepre

- 1 cup diced pancetta
- ¼ cup butter
- 2 cloves garlic, finely chopped
- salt and freshly ground black pepper
- 8 tablespoons freshly grated parmesan cheese
- 14 ounces store-bought or homemade tagliatelle (see recipe pp. 120-122)

TAGLIATELLE ALLA PANCETTA
Tagliatelle with crispy fried pancetta

Serves: 4; Preparation: 5 minutes + time needed to make the pasta; Cooking: 10-12 minutes; Level of difficulty: Simple

Sauté the pancetta, butter, and garlic over medium heat in a large skillet until the pancetta is crisp. § Cook the tagliatelle in a large pot of salted boiling water until *al dente*. Drain well and transfer to the skillet with the pancetta. Toss quickly over medium heat. Sprinkle with the parmesan and season with pepper. Serve hot.

Paglia e fieno semplice
Paglia e fieno with cream and truffles

Two types of fettuccine, the plain yellow egg variety, and the green spinach variety, are often served together. This colorful mixture is called paglia e fieno, *which means "straw and hay."*

Serves: 4; Preparation: 5 minutes; Cooking: 10 minutes; Level of difficulty: Simple

Melt the butter in a heavy-bottomed pan and add shavings of white truffle. Leave to cook for 1 minute over low heat, then add the cream. Season with salt and pepper. Simmer for 4-5 minutes or until the cream reduces. § Cook the paglia e fieno in a large pot of salted, boiling water until *al dente*. Drain well and add to the pan with the truffle sauce. Sprinkle with the parmesan and toss well over medium heat for 1-2 minutes. Serve hot.

■ INGREDIENTS

- ⅓ cup butter
- 1 large white truffle
- ¾ cup fresh cream
- salt and freshly ground black pepper
- 5 tablespoons freshly grated parmesan cheese
- 14 ounces store-bought paglia e fieno

Wine: a dry white (Pinot bianco)

Paglia e fieno alla toscana
Tuscan-style paglia e fieno

Serves: 4-6; Preparation: 30 minutes; Cooking: 45-50 minutes; Level of difficulty: Medium

Place the pancetta, prosciutto, onion, celery, and carrot in a sauté pan with half the butter and sauté over medium heat until the onion is transparent. Add the tomatoes, mushrooms, nutmeg, and salt and pepper to taste. Cook over medium heat for 15 minutes. § Add the wine and, when it has all evaporated, the peas. Simmer over medium-low heat until the peas and mushrooms are quite tender, stirring in the meat broth as needed to keep the sauce liquid enough. § Cook the paglia e fieno together in a large pot of salted, boiling water until *al dente*. Drain well and transfer to a heated serving dish. Toss vigorously with the remaining butter. Place the pasta, sauce and parmesan separately on the table so that everyone can help themselves to as much cheese and sauce as they like.

■ INGREDIENTS

- ¾ cup diced pancetta
- ½ cup diced prosciutto
- 1 large onion, 1 stalk celery, 1 large carrot, all finely chopped
- ⅓ cup butter
- 2¼ cups peeled and chopped fresh or canned tomatoes
- 4 cups coarsely chopped mushrooms
- dash of nutmeg
- salt and freshly ground black pepper
- ¾ cup dry white wine
- 3 cups fresh or frozen peas
- ¾ cup meat broth (see recipe p. 34)
- ¾ cup freshly grated parmesan cheese
- 1 pound store-bought paglia e fieno

Wine: a dry red (Chianti)

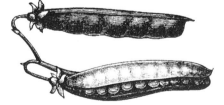

Right:
Paglia e fieno alla toscana

■ INGREDIENTS

- 1 quantity béchamel sauce
  (see recipe p. 24)
- 1 cup heavy-cream
- 2 tablespoons fresh curry
  powder
- salt and freshly ground
  black pepper
- 1 tablespoon butter
- 8 tablespoons freshly
  grated parmesan cheese
- 14 ounces store-bought
  tagliolini

Tagliolini al Curry
Tagliolini with curry sauce

Serves: 4-6; Preparation: 5 minutes; Cooking: 10 minutes; Level of difficulty: Simple

Prepare the béchamel sauce. Stir the cream and curry powder into the béchamel and cook for 2-3 more minutes. Season with salt and pepper. § Cook the tagliolini in a large pot of salted, boiling water until *al dente*. Drain well and transfer to a heated serving dish. Toss with the butter and the curry sauce. Sprinkle with parmesan and serve immediately.

Tagliatelle verdi primaverili
Spinach tagliatelle with fresh cream, peas and gorgonzola cheese

■ INGREDIENTS

• 1¼ cups fresh or frozen peas
• 3 ounces gorgonzola cheese
• 1⅓ cup fresh cream
• salt and freshly ground black pepper
• 2 tablespoons finely chopped parsley
• 8 tablespoons freshly grated parmesan cheese
• 14 ounces store-bought or homemade spinach tagliatelle (see recipe pp. 120-122)

Wine: a light, dry white (Soave)

Serves: 4; Preparation: 10 minutes + time needed to make the pasta; Cooking: 15 minutes; Level of difficulty: Simple

Cook the peas in a pot of salted, boiling water. Drain well and set aside. § Place the gorgonzola, diced into ½-inch squares, in a large heavy-bottomed pan over low heat. Stir the cheese until it melts. Stir in the cream. Add the peas and salt and pepper to taste. § Cook the pasta in a large pot of salted, boiling water until *al dente*. Drain well and transfer to the pan containing the sauce. Add the parsley and parmesan. Toss well and serve hot.

Maltagliati al ragù di agnello
Maltagliati with lamb sauce

■ INGREDIENTS

• 4 cloves garlic, finely chopped
• ⅓ cup extra-virgin olive oil
• 1 pound ground lamb
• 5 ounces ground lean pork
• 2 bay leaves
• 3 cups peeled and chopped fresh tomatoes
• 8 fresh basil leaves
• ½ teaspoon dried marjoram
• salt and freshly ground black pepper
• freshly grated pecorino cheese
• 14 ounces store-bought or homemade maltagliati (see recipe pp. 120-122)

Wine: a dry red (Rosso di Montalcino)

Maltagliati (literally "badly cut") are usually served in broth, with minestrone, or pasta soups, but they are sometimes prepared with sauces. In some Italian dialects this pasta is known as spruzzamusi, or bagnanasi, words which are difficult to translate but which mean that you are likely to get broth or sauce on your nose, cheeks and chin.

Serves: 4; Preparation: 15 minutes + time needed to make the pasta; Cooking: 1¼ hours; Level of difficulty: Simple

Sauté the garlic with the oil in a heavy-bottomed pan over a medium heat until the garlic turns light gold in color. Add the lamb, pork, and bay leaf, and sauté for 8-10 minutes. § Add the tomatoes, basil, and marjoram. Season with salt and pepper, and simmer over low heat for an hour. § Cook the maltagliati in a large pot of salted, boiling water until *al dente*. Drain, transfer to a heated serving dish, and toss with the sauce. Serve hot, with lots of pecorino for sprinkling over each portion.

Left: *Tagliatelle verdi primaverili*

TAGLIATELLE ALLA FRANTOIANA
Tagliatelle with olives and mushrooms

Serves: 4; Preparation: 10 minutes + time needed to make the pasta; Cooking: 25 minutes; Level of difficulty: Simple

Combine the garlic and parsley in a skillet with the oil and sauté until the garlic begins to change color. Add the mushrooms and cook until the water they produce has evaporated. § Add the olives, mint, salt and pepper to taste, and boiling water. Simmer for 5 minutes. § Cook the tagliatelle in a large pot of salted, boiling water until *al dente*. Drain and transfer to a heated serving dish. Toss vigorously with the sauce and serve at once.

■ INGREDIENTS

- 2 cloves garlic, finely chopped
- 3 tablespoons finely chopped parsley
- ½ cup extra-virgin olive oil
- 4 cups coarsely chopped mushrooms
- 1 cup pitted and coarsely chopped black olives
- 8 fresh mint leaves, torn
- salt and freshly ground black pepper
- ⅓ cup boiling water
- 14 ounces store-bought or homemade tagliatelle (see recipe pp. 120-122)

Wine: a dry, sparkling red (Lambrusco di Sorbara)

FETTUCCINE ALLA ROMAGNOLA
Fettuccine with simple butter and tomato sauce

The delicate taste of the fettuccine is set off by the butter-based sauce. The simplicity of the dish calls for fine homemade fettuccine. Spinach fettuccine is also good with this sauce.

Serves: 4; Preparation: 5 minutes + time needed to make the pasta; Cooking: 35 minutes; Level of difficulty: Simple

Sauté the garlic and parsley with the butter in a skillet. When the garlic begins to change color, add the tomatoes and season with salt and pepper. Simmer over medium-low heat for about 30 minutes. § Cook the fettuccine in a large pot of salted, boiling water until *al dente*. Drain well and transfer to a heated serving dish. Toss vigorously with the tomato sauce and basil. Serve hot.

■ INGREDIENTS

- 3 cloves garlic, finely chopped
- 3 tablespoons finely chopped parsley
- ½ cup butter
- 4 cups peeled and chopped ripe tomatoes
- salt and freshly ground black pepper
- 8 fresh basil leaves, torn
- 14 ounces homemade fettuccine (see recipe pp. 120-122)

Wine: a young rosé (Castel del Monte)

VARIATION
– If you are not worried about cholesterol, add a large knob of fresh butter or 2 tablespoons fresh cream to the pasta just before tossing.

Right:
Fettuccine alla romagnola

TAGLIATELLE AL SUGO D'ANATRA
Tagliatelle with duck sauce

■ INGREDIENTS

- 1 duck, cleaned and gutted, weighing about 2 pounds
- 3 tablespoons extra-virgin olive oil
- salt and freshly ground black pepper
- sprigs of fresh rosemary and sage
- 1 bay leaf
- 1 cup dry white wine
- 2 cloves garlic, 1 medium onion, 1 carrot, 1 stalk celery, all finely chopped
- 4 tablespoons tomato paste
- 5 tablespoons freshly grated pecorino cheese
- 14 ounces store-bought or homemade tagliatelle (see recipe pp. 120-122)

Serves: 4; Preparation: 20 minutes + time needed to make the pasta; Cooking: 2½ hours; Level of difficulty: Medium

Wash the duck and pat it dry with paper towels. Sprinkle with the oil, salt, pepper, rosemary, sage, and bay leaf, and roast in a preheated oven for about an hour. Turn the duck and baste it with the white wine while it is cooking. Remove from the oven and set aside. § Sauté the garlic, onion, carrot, and celery in the gravy from the roast duck until the onion is transparent. Add the tomato paste dissolved in a cup of water. Season with salt and pepper. Simmer over medium-low heat for 15 minutes. § Bone the duck and chop the meat coarsely. Add to the pan with the vegetables and cook for 45 more minutes, adding water if necessary. § Cook the tagliatelle in a large pot of salted, boiling water until *al dente*. Drain well and transfer to a heated serving bowl. Pour the sauce over the top and sprinkle with the pecorino. Toss well, and serve hot.

Wine: a dry red (Sangiovese)

TAGLIATELLE DELLA DUCHESSA
Tagliatelle with chicken-liver sauce

■ INGREDIENTS

- 9 chicken livers
- ⅔ cup butter
- 9 tablespoons freshly grated parmesan cheese
- salt and freshly ground black pepper
- 4 egg yolks
- 14 ounces store-bought or homemade tagliatelle (see recipe pp. 120-122)

This recipe comes from Emilia-Romagna in central Italy. It was named after a noblewoman Maria Luigia, Duchess of Parma, who was apparently very fond of it.

Serves: 4; Preparation: 1¼ hours + time needed to make the pasta; Cooking: 15 minutes; Level of difficulty: Medium

Soak the chicken livers for 1 hour in a large bowl of cold water. § Chop the livers finely. Place in a skillet with the butter and cook over medium-low heat for 8-10 minutes. Season with salt and pepper. § Cook the tagliatelle in a large pot of salted, boiling water until *al dente*. Drain well and transfer to a heated serving dish. § Add the chicken livers, parmesan, and egg yolks. Toss well. The egg yolks shouldn't cook but form a soft creamy sauce. Serve hot.

Wine: a dry red (Cabernet)

■ INGREDIENTS

- ⅓ cup butter
- 1¼ cups heavy cream
- 8 tablespoons freshly grated parmesan cheese
- dash of nutmeg
- salt and freshly ground black pepper
- 14 ounces store-bought or homemade tagliatelle (see recipe pp. 120-122)

FETTUCCINE ALL'ALFREDO
Fettuccine with butter and cream sauce

Serves: 4; Preparation: 5 minutes + time needed to make the pasta; Cooking: 10 minutes; Level of difficulty: Simple

Place the butter and cream in a heavy-bottomed pan and cook over high heat for 2 minutes. Remove from heat. § Cook the fettuccine in a large pot of salted, boiling water until *al dente*. Drain well and transfer to the pan with the cream. Add the parmesan, nutmeg, salt and pepper to taste, and place over medium-low heat for 1 minute, tossing the pasta constantly. Serve immediately.

Filled Pasta

Filled pasta is made by wrapping small quantities
of meat or vegetable stuffing in delicious fresh, egg pasta.
The various types of ravioli, tortellini, and tortelli are
usually served with classic ragù, or simple cream, butter,
and herb sauces that won't camouflage the delicate taste
of the pasta and filling.

Agnolotti in brodo
Agnolotti in meat broth

Agnolotti are a specialty of the Piedmont region in northern Italy. They are square in shape, like tortelli. They are usually stuffed with meat-based fillings and can be served in meat broth or meat sauces as shown here. They are also good with simple butter and sage sauce (see recipe p. 24), or butter and parmesan sauce (see recipe p. 24).

Serves: 4-6; Preparation: 30 minutes + time needed to make the pasta; Cooking: 15 minutes + 3 hours for the broth; Level of difficulty: Medium

Make the pasta dough. § Combine the onion, celery, carrot, and garlic with the butter in a heavy-bottomed pan and sauté over medium heat. When the onion turns light gold, add the pork, veal, liver, and bay leaf. Sauté for a few minutes, then add the wine. Cover and simmer over low heat for about 10 minutes, or until the meat is cooked. Remove the meat from the pan. § Put the cooked meat in a blender or food processor and chop finely. Transfer to a mixing bowl. § When cool, add the egg, parmesan, nutmeg, and season with salt and pepper. § Prepare the agnolotti as shown on p. 123. § Place the agnolotti in a large pot of boiling meat broth and cook until the pasta around the sealed edges is *al dente*. Transfer the agnolotti and meat broth to a large heated soup dish and serve hot.

■ INGREDIENTS

PASTA: see recipe pp. 120-123
FILLING
- 1 small onion, 1 stalk celery, 1 small carrot, 1 clove garlic, all finely chopped
- ¼ cup butter
- 5 ounces lean pork, 5 ounces lean veal, 3½ ounces liver, all coarsely chopped
- 1 bay leaf
- 1 cup dry red wine
- 1 large egg
- 2 tablespoons freshly grated parmesan cheese
- dash of nutmeg
- salt and freshly ground black pepper

MEAT BROTH: see recipe p. 34

Wine: a dry red (Grignolino)

Agnolotti con sugo di carne
Agnolotti with meat sauce

Serves: 4-6; Preparation: 30 minutes + time needed to make the pasta; Cooking: 15 minutes + time needed to make the meat sauce; Level of difficulty: Medium

Make the pasta dough. § Prepare the agnolotti filling as shown above. § Prepare the agnolotti as shown on p. 123. § Prepare the meat sauce. § Cook the agnolotti in a large pot of salted, boiling water until the pasta round the sealed edges is *al dente*. Remove from the water using a slotted spoon and place on a heated serving dish. Cover with the hot meat sauce. Sprinkle with the parmesan and, if you have them, shavings of white truffle. Serve hot.

■ INGREDIENTS

PASTA: see recipe pp. 120-123
FILLING: see above
MEAT SAUCE: see recipe p. 26
- 4 tablespoons freshly grated parmesan cheese
- white truffle (optional)

Wine: a dry red (Dolcetto)

Right:
Agnolotti in brodo

Ravioli semplici al burro

Ravioli with Italian sausage filling in butter and sage sauce

Serves: 4-6; Preparation: 20 minutes + time needed to make the pasta; Cooking: 10 minutes; Level of difficulty: Medium

Make the pasta dough. § Cook the spinach and chard in a pot of salted water until tender (3-4 minutes if frozen, 8-10 minutes if fresh). Squeeze out excess moisture and chop finely. § Mix the sausages, ricotta, eggs, parmesan, and marjoram with the spinach and chard in a mixing bowl. Combine thoroughly and season with salt. § Prepare the ravioli as shown on p. 123. § Cook in a large pot of salted, boiling water until the sealed edges of the ravioli are *al dente*. Drain and transfer to a heated serving dish. While the ravioli are cooking, prepare the sauce. Pour over ravioli and sprinkle with extra grated parmesan.

> VARIATION
> – *Ravioli semplici* are also very good with meat sauce (see recipe p. 26) or tomato and butter sauce (see recipe p. 22).

■ INGREDIENTS

PASTA: see recipe pp. 120-123
FILLING
- 6 ounces fresh or 4 ounces frozen spinach
- 1¼ pounds fresh or 12 ounces frozen chard
- 8 ounces Italian pork sausages, skinned and crumbled
- ¾ cup fresh ricotta cheese
- 2 eggs
- 3 tablespoons freshly grated parmesan cheese
- ½ teaspoon dried marjoram
- salt
BUTTER AND SAGE SAUCE: see recipe p. 24

Wine: a dry red (Freisa)

Ravioli verdi al pomodoro

Spinach ravioli with ricotta cheese filling in tomato sauce

Serves: 4-6; Preparation: 30 minutes + time needed to make the pasta; Cooking: 10 minutes; Level of difficulty: Medium

Make the spinach pasta dough. § Place the ricotta in a mixing bowl. Add the parsley, basil, eggs, nutmeg, and salt to taste. Combine the ingredients thoroughly and set aside. § Prepare the tomato and butter sauce. § Prepare the ravioli as shown on p. 123. § Cook in a large pot of salted, boiling water until the sealed edges of the ravioli are *al dente*. Drain well and transfer to a heated serving dish. Pour the hot tomato sauce over the ravioli and toss gently. Sprinkle with parmesan and serve hot.

■ INGREDIENTS

PASTA: see recipe pp. 120-123
FILLING
- 1 cup fresh ricotta cheese
- 2½ cups parsley and 3 cups fresh basil, finely chopped
- 2 eggs
- ¼ teaspoon nutmeg
- salt
- 4 tablespoons freshly grated parmesan cheese
TOMATO AND BUTTER SAUCE: see recipe p. 22

Right: Ravioli semplici al burro

■ INGREDIENTS

PASTA: see recipe pp. 120-123

FILLING

- 1¾ cups fresh ricotta cheese
- 2 eggs
- ¼ teaspoon nutmeg
- 4 tablespoons freshly grated parmesan cheese
- salt

BUTTER AND SAGE SAUCE: see recipe p. 24

Wine: a dry white (Frascati)

RAVIOLI DI RICOTTA AL BURRO E SALVIA
Ravioli with ricotta filling in butter and sage sauce

Serves: 4-6; Preparation: 10 minutes + time needed to make the pasta; Cooking: 10 minutes; Level of difficulty: Medium

Make the pasta dough. § Place the ricotta in a mixing bowl and add eggs, nutmeg, parmesan, and salt to taste. Combine thoroughly. § Prepare the ravioli as shown on p. 123. § Cook the ravioli in a large pot of salted, boiling water until the pasta around the sealed edges is *al dente*. Drain well and transfer to a heated serving dish. Cover with the sage sauce and extra grated parmesan. Toss gently and serve hot.

Ingredients

■ INGREDIENTS

PASTA: see recipe pp. 120-123

FILLING

- 2 ounces boneless lean pork, 2 ounces chicken breast, coarsely chopped
- ¼ cup butter
- 2 ounces prosciutto, 4 ounces mortadella, finely chopped
- 2 eggs
- 6 tablespoons freshly grated parmesan cheese
- ¼ teaspoon nutmeg
- salt and freshly ground black pepper

SAUCE

- ½ cup butter
- 1 cup fresh cream
- 1 medium truffle, white or black
- 8 tablespoons freshly grated parmesan cheese

Wine: a dry white (Orvieto)

■ INGREDIENTS

PASTA: see recipe pp. 120-123

FILLING: see recipe above

SAUCE

- 2 cups fresh or frozen peas
- 5 cups coarsely chopped mushrooms
- 2 cloves garlic, finely chopped
- 3 tablespoons finely chopped parsley
- 4 tablespoons extra-virgin olive oil
- 2 14-ounce cans tomatoes
- salt and freshly ground black pepper

Wine: a dry red (Sangiovese)

Left: *Tortellini alla panna* and *Tortellini alla boscaiola*

TORTELLINI ALLA PANNA
Tortellini with cream sauce

Serves: 4-6; Preparation: 25 minutes + time needed to make the pasta; Cooking: 10 minutes; Level of difficulty: Medium

Make the pasta dough. § Put the pork and chicken in a sauté pan with the butter and sauté over medium heat for about 5 minutes, or until tender. Remove from the pan and chop finely in a food processor. § Sauté prosciutto and mortadella in the same pan for 2-3 minutes. § Combine pork, chicken, prosciutto, and mortadella in a mixing bowl. Add the eggs, parmesan, nutmeg, and salt and pepper to taste, and mix thoroughly. Set aside. § Prepare the tortellini as shown on p. 123. § Cook the tortellini in a large pot of salted, boiling water until the sealed edges of the pasta are *al dente*. § To make the sauce, melt the butter in a large saucepan over low heat. Stir in the cream and cook for 2-3 minutes. § When the tortellini are cooked, drain well and transfer to the pan with the cream. Add the parmesan, shavings of truffle, salt and pepper to taste, and toss gently over medium-low heat for 2-3 minutes. Serve hot.

TORTELLINI ALLA BOSCAIOLA
Tortellini with woodsmen-style sauce

Serves: 4-6; Preparation: 25 minutes + time needed to make the pasta; Cooking: 35 minutes; Level of difficulty: Medium

Make the pasta dough. § Make the tortellini filling and set aside. § Cook the peas in boiling water. Drain and set aside. § Put the mushrooms, garlic, and parsley in a large sauté pan with the oil and cook for 5 minutes, or until the water the mushrooms produce has evaporated. Add the tomatoes and simmer for about 20 minutes. Add the cooked peas and salt and pepper to taste. Cook for 3-4 more minutes. § While the sauce is cooking, prepare the tortellini as shown on p. 123. § Cook in a large pot of salted, boiling water until sealed pasta edges are *al dente*. Drain well and transfer to the sauté pan. Toss gently and serve immediately.

TORTELLI DI PATATE AL BURRO E SALVIA
Tortelli with potato filling
in butter and sage sauce

■ INGREDIENTS

PASTA: see recipe pp. 120-123
FILLING
• 1¼ pounds potatoes
• 1 medium onion
• ¼ cup butter
• 6 tablespoons freshly
   grated parmesan cheese
• 3 eggs
• ¼ teaspoon nutmeg
• freshly ground black
   pepper
BUTTER AND SAGE SAUCE:
   see recipe p. 24

Wine: a light, young dry white
(Riesling dell'Oltrepò Pavese)

Serves: 4-6; Preparation: 40 minutes + time needed to make the pasta; Cooking: 10-15 minutes;
Level of difficulty: Medium

Make the pasta dough. § Peel the potatoes and cook them in salted, boiling water. § Put the onion and butter in a large sauté pan and cook until the onion begins to change color. § Mash the potatoes in a mixing bowl and add the onion, half the parmesan, the eggs, nutmeg and a pinch of pepper. Mix thoroughly and set aside to cool. § Prepare the tortelli as shown on p. 123. § Cook the tortelli in a large pot of salted, boiling water until the sealed edges of the pasta are *al dente*. Drain well and transfer to a heated serving dish. § Make the butter and sage sauce and pour over the tortelli. Sprinkle with parmesan and serve hot.

VARIATION
– Potato tortelli are also delicious with meat sauce (see recipe
p. 26).

TORTELLI CON LE BIETE
Tortelli with chard filling
in butter and parmesan sauce

■ INGREDIENTS

PASTA: see recipe pp. 120-123
FILLING
• 1 pound fresh or 11
   ounces frozen chard
• ¾ cup fresh ricotta
   cheese
• ⅔ cup mascarpone cheese

Serves: 4-6; Preparation: 45 minutes + time needed to make the pasta; Cooking: 10-15 minutes;
Level of difficulty: Medium

Make the pasta dough. § Cook the chard in a pot of salted water until tender (3-4 minutes if frozen, 8-10 minutes if fresh). Drain well and squeeze out any extra moisture. Chop finely and place in a mixing bowl. Add the ricotta, mascarpone, parmesan, eggs, and nutmeg. Mix

Right:
Tortelli con le biete

- 6 tablespoons freshly
  grated parmesan cheese
- 2 eggs
- ¼ teaspoon nutmeg
- salt

BUTTER AND PARMESAN
  SAUCE: see recipe p. 24

thoroughly and add salt to taste. § Prepare the tortelli as shown on p. 123. § Cook the tortelli in a large pot of salted, boiling water until the sealed edges of the pasta are *al dente*. Drain well and transfer to a heated serving dish. Cover with the sauce, toss gently, and serve immediately.

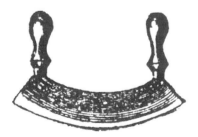

Wine: a dry red
(Brachetto d'Acqui)

Ravioli alle zucchine
Ravioli with zucchini filling in butter and rosemary sauce

Serves: 4-6; Preparation: 30 minutes + time needed to make the pasta; Cooking: 10 minutes; Level of difficulty: Medium

Make the pasta dough. § Cook the zucchini in a pot of salted, boiling water until tender. Drain, transfer to a bowl, and mash finely with a fork. Add the amaretti, ricotta, parmesan, and nutmeg. Season with salt. Mix well to form a thick cream. If the filling is too liquid, add dry bread crumbs; if it is too thick add a little milk. § Prepare the ravioli as shown on p. 123. § Cook in a large pot of salted, boiling water until the sealed edges of the pasta are *al dente*. Drain well and transfer to a heated serving dish. § While the pasta is cooking, prepare the sauce. Place the garlic in a small saucepan with the butter and rosemary and cook for 3-4 minutes over medium heat, stirring frequently. § Pour the sauce over the ravioli, sprinkle with the parmesan, and serve immediately.

■ INGREDIENTS

PASTA: see recipe pp. 120-123
FILLING
• 2 medium zucchini
• ¾ cup crushed amaretti biscuits
• ⅔ cup fresh ricotta cheese
• ¾ cup freshly grated parmesan cheese
• ¼ teaspoon nutmeg
• salt
• 4 tablespoons freshly grated parmesan cheese
SAUCE
• 2 cloves garlic, finely chopped
• ½ cup butter
• 4 tablespoons finely chopped rosemary

Wine: a dry white (Pinot Bianco)

Agnolini con ripieno di pollo al brodo
Agnolini with chicken filling in chicken broth

Agnolini *are also known as* agnoli, cappelletti *and* marubini. *The name used in Emilia-Romagna,* cappelletti *("little hats") comes closest to describing their shape. These chicken-filled agnolini served with chicken broth are light and easy to digest.*

Serves: 4-6; Preparation: 35 minutes + time needed to make the pasta; Cooking: 10 minutes; Level of difficulty: Medium

Make the pasta dough. § Boil the chicken breasts in chicken or meat broth until tender. § Chop finely using a knife or in a food processor. Transfer to a mixing bowl and add eggs, parmesan, nutmeg, and salt to taste. Mix thoroughly. § Prepare the agnolini as shown on p. 123. § Cook in a large pot of boiling chicken broth until the sealed edges of the pasta are *al dente*. Transfer to a heated serving dish with the broth and serve hot.

■ INGREDIENTS

PASTA: see recipe pp. 120-123
FILLING
• 2 boneless, skinless chicken breasts
• 3 eggs
• ¾ cup freshly grated parmesan cheese
• ¼ teaspoon nutmeg
• salt
BROTH: see recipe p. 34

Wine: a light, dry red (Lambrusco)

VARIATION
– Also good with butter and parmesan sauce (see recipe p. 24), tomato and butter sauce (see recipe p. 22), and meat sauce (see recipe p. 26).

Right: *Agnolini con ripieno di pollo al brodo*

Ravioli di pesce con salsa di verdure
Ravioli with fish filling in vegetable sauce

Serves: 4-6; Preparation: 1 hour + time needed to make the pasta; Cooking: 15 minutes; Level of difficulty: Complicated

Make the pasta dough. § Melt the butter in a skillet. Add the fish fillets and cook over medium heat for 5 minutes, or until tender. Chop the cooked fish very finely with a knife or in a food processor. § Cook the chard in a pot of salted water until tender (3-4 minutes if frozen, 8-10 minutes if fresh). Squeeze out excess moisture and chop finely. § Combine the fish and chard in a bowl with the ricotta, eggs, parmesan, and nutmeg. Add salt to taste and mix well. § Prepare the ravioli as shown on p. 123. Set aside. § Put the mushrooms in a small bowl of warm water and leave for 10 minutes. Remove from the water and chop finely. Combine the vegetables with the butter in the sauté pan used to cook the fish, add the tomatoes and a cup of water, and cook over medium-low heat for 20 minutes. Add salt to taste. § Roast the pine nuts in the oven with the flour, and chop finely in a food processor. Add to the tomato sauce. § Cook the ravioli in a large pot of salted, boiling water until the sealed edges of the pasta are *al dente*. Drain well and transfer to a heated serving dish. Pour the sauce over the top, sprinkle with parmesan, and serve immediately.

Tortelloni valdostani
Tortelloni with veal, spinach and rosemary filling in cheese sauce

Tortelloni are the same shape as tortellini only larger.
This dish comes from the Val d'Aosta, near the French border in northern Italy.

Serves: 4-6; Preparation: 1½ hours + time needed to make the pasta; Cooking: 5-8 minutes; Level of difficulty: Medium

Make the pasta dough. § Place the rosemary in a sauté pan with the butter and sauté for 2-3 minutes. Add the veal and white wine, and simmer over medium-low heat. When the veal is tender, remove from the

---

■ INGREDIENTS

PASTA: see recipe pp. 120-123
FILLING

- ¼ cup butter
- 14 ounces bass fillets
- 12 ounces fresh or 6½ ounces frozen chard
- ¼ cup fresh ricotta cheese
- 2 eggs
- 6 tablespoons freshly grated parmesan cheese
- ¼ teaspoon nutmeg
- salt

SAUCE

- 2½ tablespoons dried mushrooms
- 1 stalk celery, 1 medium onion, 1 tablespoon parsley, all finely chopped
- ½ cup butter
- 4 ripe tomatoes, peeled and chopped
- salt
- 3 tablespoons pine nuts
- ¾ tablespoon all-purpose flour
- 8 tablespoons freshly grated parmesan cheese

Wine: a dry white (Cinque Terre)

■ INGREDIENTS

PASTA: see recipe pp. 120-123
FILLING

- 1 tablespoon finely chopped fresh rosemary
- ¼ cup butter
- 10 ounces lean veal
- 2 tablespoons dry white wine
- 8 ounces fresh or 5 ounces frozen spinach
- 1 egg and 1 egg yolk

- 4 tablespoons freshly
  grated parmesan cheese
- dash of nutmeg
- salt and freshly ground
  black pepper

SAUCE
- 6 ounces fontina cheese
- ¼ cup butter
- ½ teaspoon nutmeg

Above: *Tortelloni valdostani*

pan and chop finely with a knife or in a food processor. § Cook the spinach in a pot of salted water until tender (3-4 minutes if frozen, 8-10 minutes if fresh). Squeeze out excess moisture and chop finely. § Combine the veal and spinach in a bowl and add the eggs, parmesan and nutmeg. Season with salt and pepper. Mix well with a fork and set aside for 1 hour. § Prepare the tortelloni as shown on p. 123. § Cook the tortelloni in a large pot of salted, boiling water until the sealed edges of the pasta are *al dente*. Drain well and transfer to a heated serving dish. § While the pasta is cooking, prepare the sauce. Combine the cheese, butter, and nutmeg in a small saucepan over very low heat until the cheese is melted. Pour over the tortelloni and serve hot.

Baked Pasta

Baked pasta dishes are hearty fare, well-suited to cold winter evenings. Lasagna is the classic baked pasta dish, but there are many others. Most baked dishes are based on precooked pasta combined with béchamel, tomato, or meat sauces, sprinkled with tasty parmesan cheese which forms a golden crust in the oven.

Lasagne al forno
Lasagne with Bolognese meat sauce

■ INGREDIENTS

MEAT SAUCE: see recipe
p. 26

PASTA: 1 pound store-
bought dried lasagne
sheets or 1 quantity
homemade lasagne.
See recipe p. 120

• butter to grease the
baking dish and for the
crust
• 1 cup freshly grated
parmesan cheese

BÉCHAMEL: see recipe p. 24

Wine: a dry red
(Sangiovese)

Serves: 4–6; Preparation: 30 minutes + time needed to make the pasta and the sauce; Cooking: 20 minutes; Level of difficulty: Complicated

Prepare the meat sauce. § Make the pasta dough and prepare the lasagne. § Prepare a large pot of salted, boiling water. Cook the lasagne 4-5 sheets at a time for about 1½ minutes. Remove with a slotted spoon, plunge into a bowl of cold water to stop the cooking process. Remove quickly, and rinse gently under cold running water. Lay the sheets out separately on dry dishcloths and pat dry. § Prepare the béchamel and combine with the meat sauce. § Smear the bottom of a large oblong baking dish with butter to prevent the lasagne from sticking. Line with a single layer of cooked lasagne sheets. Cover with a thin layer of meat and béchamel sauce. Sprinkle with grated parmesan, then add another layer of lasagne. Repeat until you have at least 6 layers. Leave enough sauce to spread a thin layer on top. Sprinkle with parmesan and add knobs of butter here and there. § Bake in a preheated oven at 400° F for 15-20 minutes. A crust should form on the top. Serve hot.

VARIATIONS
– For *Lasagne with mushroom sauce* follow the instructions above, replacing the meat sauce with mushroom sauce (see recipe p. 30).
– For *Lasagne with Genoese basil sauce* follow the instructions above, replacing the meat sauce with basil sauce (see recipe p. 28).

Rigatoni giganti farciti
Rigatoni giganti filled with meat sauce

■ INGREDIENTS

• 1 quantity meat sauce (see
recipe p. 26)
• 1¼ cups chopped
mushrooms
• ¼ cup butter
• 10 ounces ground lean
beef
• 1 egg
• ½ tablespoon all-purpose
flour

You will need a piping bag and tip or syringe to get the filling into the rigatoni.

Serves: 4; Preparation: 35 minutes + time needed to make the sauce; Cooking: 15 minutes; Level of difficulty: Medium

Prepare the meat sauce. § Cook the rigatoni in a large pot of salted, boiling water for half the cooking time indicated on the package. Drain well and place on dry dishcloths. § Place the mushrooms and half the butter in a sauté pan and cook over medium-low heat for about 10 minutes, or until the mushrooms are tender. § Combine the mushrooms

Right:
Rigatoni giganti farciti

- 4 tablespoons dry white wine
- 1 tablespoon tomato paste, dissolved in 1 cup hot water
- salt and freshly ground black pepper
- 8 tablespoons freshly grated parmesan cheese
- 14 ounces rigatoni giganti

Wine: a dry red
(Chianti dei Colli Fiorentini)

with the beef, half the meat sauce, the egg, flour, and wine in a heavy-bottomed pan. Mix well. Add all but 1 tablespoon of the tomato and water mixture. Season with salt and pepper. Cover, and cook over medium-low heat for about 15 minutes, stirring frequently with a wooden spoon. Remove from heat. § Fill the piping bag with the mixture and stuff the rigatoni one by one. § Grease an ovenproof dish with butter and place the filled rigatoni in it. Mix the remaining tomato mixture and meat sauce together and pour over the top. Sprinkle with the grated parmesan and dot with the remaining butter. § Bake in a preheated oven at 350° F for 15 minutes or until a golden crust has formed on top. Serve hot in the ovenproof dish.

INGREDIENTS

- 2 cloves garlic, finely chopped
- 2 tablespoons finely chopped parsley
- 8 fresh basil leaves, torn
- ⅓ cup extra-virgin olive oil
- 2 14-ounce cans tomatoes, chopped
- ½ teaspoon crushed chilies
- salt and freshly ground black pepper
- 5 ounces mozzarella cheese, thinly sliced
- 6 tablespoons freshly grated pecorino cheese
- 14 ounces fusilli

Wine: a dry red (Oltrepò Pavese)

INGREDIENTS

SAUCE
- ½ quantity tomato and butter sauce (see recipe p. 22)
- 1 quantity béchamel (see recipe p. 24)

FILLING
- 1 pound fresh or 11 ounces frozen spinach
- ¼ cup butter
- 1¼ cups fresh ricotta cheese
- ¾ cup freshly grated parmesan cheese
- 2 eggs
- salt and freshly ground black pepper
- 12 store-bought cannelloni, spinach or plain

Wine: a light, dry red (Vino Novello)

Left:
Cannelloni di ricotta e spinaci

FUSILLI CON MOZZARELLA E POMODORO
Fusilli with tomatoes and mozzarella cheese

Serves: 4; Preparation: 30 minutes; Cooking: 30 minutes; Level of difficulty: Simple

Combine the garlic, parsley, and basil with the oil in a skillet and cook over medium heat until the garlic begins to change color. Add the tomatoes and chilies. Season with salt and pepper. Stir well and simmer over low heat for about 20 minutes, or until sauce has reduced. § Cook the fusilli in a large pot of salted, boiling water for half the time recommended on the package. Drain thoroughly and combine with the tomato sauce. Transfer the mixture to a greased baking dish and arrange the mozzarella over the top. Sprinkle with the pecorino. § Bake in a preheated oven at 350° F for about 30 minutes, or until the cheese is lightly browned.

CANNELLONI DI RICOTTA E SPINACI
Cannelloni with ricotta and spinach filling in tomato and béchamel sauce

Serves: 4-6; Preparation: 40 minutes; Cooking: 20 minutes; Level of difficulty: Medium

Prepare the tomato sauce. § Cook the spinach in a pot of salted water until tender (3-4 minutes if frozen, 8-10 minutes if fresh). Drain, squeeze out excess moisture and chop finely. § Put half the butter in a skillet with the spinach. Season with salt and pepper. Cook briefly over high heat until the spinach has absorbed the flavor of the butter. § Transfer to a bowl and mix well with the ricotta, half the parmesan and the eggs. § Prepare the béchamel. § Cook the cannelloni in a large pot of salted, boiling water until half-cooked (about 5 minutes). Drain, and pass the colander with the pasta under cold running water. Dry the cannelloni with paper towels and stuff with the ricotta and spinach. § Line the bottom of an ovenproof dish with a layer of béchamel and place the cannelloni in a single layer on it. Cover with alternate spoonfuls of béchamel and tomato sauce. Sprinkle with the remaining parmesan and dot with butter. § Cook at 400° F for about 20 minutes or until a golden crust has formed on the top. Serve hot.

VARIATION
– Replace tomato sauce with 1 quantity of meat sauce (see recipe p. 26).

Penne Gratinate al Forno
Baked penne rigate

Serves: 4; Preparation: 30 minutes; Cooking: 30 minutes; Level of difficulty: Simple

Sauté the parsley, onion, and garlic with the oil in a skillet until lightly browned. Add the tomatoes and simmer over low heat for 25 minutes. § Cook the penne in a large pot of salted, boiling water for half the time shown on the package. Drain well. § Place a layer of pasta in a greased baking dish. Cover with a layer of pancetta, tomato mixture, and both cheeses. Repeat layers until the dish is full, reserving a little of both cheeses to sprinkle on top. They will turn golden brown in the oven. Bake in a preheated oven at 350° F for 30 minutes and serve piping hot.

■ INGREDIENTS

- 4 tablespoons parsley, 1 large onion, 2 cloves garlic, all finely chopped
- ¼ cup extra-virgin olive oil
- 3 cups peeled and diced ripe tomatoes
- salt and freshly ground black pepper
- 1½ cups diced pancetta
- 2 cups diced mozzarella cheese
- 1 cup freshly grated pecorino cheese
- 14 ounces penne rigate

Wine: a dry red (Valpolicella)

Maccheroni Incaciati

Maccheroni baked with veal, salame, eggs, mozzarella cheese and vegetables

Serves: 4-6; Preparation: 1½ hours; Cooking 20 minutes; Level of difficulty: Simple

To take away the harsh taste of the eggplants, sprinkle each slice with salt and place in a large bowl. Cover, and set aside for an hour. § Put the slices on a cutting board and remove the peel with a knife. Rinse under cold running water and pat dry with paper towels. § Dust the slices with flour. Heat the vegetable oil in a large skillet until very hot and add the eggplant. Sauté until golden brown on both sides. Remove from the pan and place on a platter covered with paper towels. § Grease a deep-sided ovenproof dish with a little oil and line the bottom with slices of fried eggplant. § Cook the garlic in a large sauté pan with the olive oil until it begins to change color. Add the tomatoes, veal, salame, peas, and basil and simmer over medium-low heat for about 30 minutes, stirring occasionally with a wooden spoon. Add the chopped chicken livers and cook for 5 more minutes. § Cook the maccheroni in a large pot of salted, boiling water for half the cooking time indicated on the package. Drain well. § Mix with the sauce, eggs, and any remaining eggplant slices. Pour into the baking dish with the eggplant. Cover with the sliced mozzarella and grated pecorino. Bake in a preheated oven at 400° F for about 20 minutes, or until a golden crust has formed on top. Serve hot in the baking dish.

■ INGREDIENTS

- 2 medium eggplants, cut lengthwise into ¼-inch thick slices
- salt and freshly ground black pepper
- 4 tablespoons all-purpose flour
- vegetable oil for frying
- 1 clove garlic, chopped
- 4 tablespoons extra-virgin olive oil
- 1 14-ounce can tomatoes
- 1 cup coarsely chopped veal
- ⅔ cup diced salame
- ⅔ cup fresh or frozen peas
- 4 basil leaves, torn
- ¾ cup coarsely chopped chicken livers
- 2 hard-cooked eggs, cut in quarters
- 1¼ cups mozzarella cheese
- 4 tablespoons freshly grated pecorino cheese
- 14 ounces maccheroni

Right: Penne gratinate al forno

Timballo di maccheroni alla ferrarese
Maccheroni with meat sauce, béchamel and truffles baked in pastry casing

■ INGREDIENTS

MEAT SAUCE: see recipe
p. 26

BÉCHAMEL: see recipe p. 24

PASTRY: see recipe for
Timballo di gnocchi
p. 110

• 1½ tablespoons butter
• 2 tablespoons bread
crumbs
• 1 whole white truffle
• 1 cup freshly grated
parmesan cheese
• 1 pound maccheroni

*Wine: a dry red
(Barbaresco)*

Serves: 4-6; Preparation: 30 minutes + time needed to make sauces; Cooking: 30 minutes; Level of difficulty: Complicated

Prepare 1 quantity of meat sauce and a ½ quantity of béchamel. § Prepare the pastry dough. § Cook the maccheroni in a large pot of salted, boiling water for half the time indicated on the package. Drain well and mix with half the meat sauce. § Grease an ovenproof baking dish with butter and sprinkle with finely ground bread crumbs. Roll the dough out to about ⅛ inch thick and line the baking dish. Line the bottom with a layer of béchamel, then cover with pasta and meat sauce. Sprinkle with fine shavings of truffle. Repeat until all the ingredients are in the baking dish. The last layer should be of béchamel. Sprinkle with the parmesan. § Bake in a preheated oven at 350° F for about 30 minutes. Serve hot.

Strudel di spinaci al forno
Baked spinach and ricotta roll

■ INGREDIENTS

PASTA: see recipe pp. 120-121

FILLING
• 1¾ pounds fresh or 1
pound frozen spinach
• 1 cup fresh ricotta cheese
• 3 tablespoons freshly
grated parmesan cheese
• ¼ teaspoon nutmeg
• salt

Serves: 4-6; Preparation: 1 hour; Cooking: 45 minutes; Level of difficulty: Complicated

Make the pasta. § Cook the spinach in a pot of salted water until tender (3-4 minutes if frozen, 8-10 minutes if fresh). Drain, squeeze out excess moisture and chop finely. § Put the spinach in a bowl and add the ricotta, parmesan, and nutmeg. Combine thoroughly and season with salt. § Lightly flour a table top or flat work surface and roll the pasta dough out until it is very thin. Cut the dough into a 12 by 16-inch rectangle. § Spread the spinach and ricotta mixture evenly over the top and roll it up. Seal the ends by squeezing the dough together. Wrap

Right:
Strudel di spinaci al forno

BÉCHAMEL: see recipe p. 24

TOMATO AND BUTTER
SAUCE: see recipe p. 22

*Wine: a dry red
(Collio Merlot)*

the roll tightly in cheesecloth, tying the ends with string. § Bring a large pot of salted water to a boil. The pot should be wide enough so that the roll can lie flat. Immerse the roll carefully into the boiling water and simmer for about 20 minutes. Remove from the pot and set aside. § While the roll is cooking, prepare half quantities of béchamel and tomato sauces. § Unwrap the spinach roll and cut into slices about ½ inch thick. Cover the bottom of an ovenproof dish with a layer of béchamel and top with slices of spinach roll. Mix the remaining béchamel with the tomato sauce and cover the spinach slices. Sprinkle with extra parmesan and bake in a preheated oven at 350° F for about 15 minutes, or until a golden crust forms on top. Serve hot.

PASTICCIO DI MALTAGLIATI AL PROSCIUTTO
Baked maltagliati with ham, cream and eggs

Serves: 4; Preparation: 15 minutes; Cooking: 1 hour; Level of difficulty: Medium

Melt the butter in a saucepan over low heat. Add the egg yolks, ham, and parsley, and stir with a wooden spoon for 2-3 minutes. Add the nutmeg and season with salt and pepper. Remove from heat. § Whip the cream until stiff. In a separate bowl, beat the egg whites until stiff. Gently stir the whipped cream into the egg whites and add to the butter mixture. § Cook the pasta in a large pot of salted, boiling water for half the recommended time. Drain well and place on dry dishcloths. § Grease an ovenproof dish with butter and place the pasta in it. Cover with the egg, cream and ham mixture. Sprinkle with the parmesan cheese. Bake in a preheated oven at 350° F for about 50 minutes. Serve in the ovenproof dish.

VARIATION
– Replace the cream and egg whites with 1 quantity of béchamel sauce (see recipe p. 24).

■ INGREDIENTS

- ¼ cup butter
- 4 eggs, separated
- 1½ cups finely chopped boiled ham
- 2 tablespoons finely chopped parsley
- dash of nutmeg
- salt and freshly ground black pepper
- 1 cup fresh cream
- 8 tablespoons freshly grated parmesan cheese
- 14 ounces store-bought dried maltagliati

Wine: a dry red (Chianti Classico)

POMODORI RIPIENI DI PASTA
Baked tomatoes with pasta filling

Choose firm, red tomatoes with their stalks still attached for this tasty, baked tomato dish. The tomatoes can be served hot straight from the oven or left to cool and served as a cold entrée.

Serves: 4; Preparation: 20 minutes; Cooking: 40 minutes; Level of difficulty: Simple

Rinse the tomatoes and dry well. Cut the top off each tomato (with its stalk) and set aside. Hollow out the insides of the bottom parts with a teaspoon. Put the pulp in a bowl. § Place a basil leaf in the bottom of each hollow shell. § Cook the pasta in a medium pot of salted, boiling water for half the time indicated on the package. Drain well. § Combine the pasta with the tomato mixture. Add the parsley and 2 tablespoons of the oil. Season with salt and pepper. § Stuff the hollow tomatoes with the mixture. § Grease an ovenproof dish with the remaining oil and carefully place the tomatoes on it. Cover with the tomato tops. § Bake for about 40 minutes in a preheated oven at 350° F. Serve either hot or cold.

■ INGREDIENTS

- 8 medium tomatoes
- 8 basil leaves
- 2 tablespoons finely chopped parsley
- 3 tablespoons extra-virgin olive oil
- salt and freshly ground black pepper
- 8 tablespoons ditaloni rigati or other small, tubular pasta

Wine: a dry white (Frascati)

Right:
Pomodori ripieni di pasta

GNOCCHI

The most common type of gnocchi are the white
potato ones, made with mashed potatoes and flour.
But there are also spinach gnocchi, ricotta gnocchi,
baked semolina gnocchi, and fried gnocchi.

Gnocchi di patate al gorgonzola

Potato gnocchi with gorgonzola cheese sauce

Potato gnocchi are a simple mixture of boiled, mashed potatoes and flour. They are made in the same way throughout Italy, although in some regions eggs are added to the basic dough. The choice of potato is important. Don't use new potatoes or baking potatoes; the humble boiling potato is best. Besides the cheese-based sauces given below, potato gnocchi are also good with tomato and butter sauce (see p. 22), pesto (see p. 28), and meat sauce (see p. 26).

Serves: 6; Preparation: 20 minutes; Cooking: 35 minutes; Level of difficulty: Medium

Cook the potatoes in their skins in a pot of salted, boiling water for 20 minutes, or until tender. Drain and peel while still hot. Mash until smooth. Place on a flat work surface and add most of the flour. Knead the mixture, adding more flour as required, until it is soft and smooth, but just slightly sticky. The amount of flour required will depend on how much the potatoes can absorb, so don't add it all at once. § Dust the work surface with flour, take a piece of the dough and roll it into a long sausage about ¾ inch in diameter. Cut into pieces about 1 inch in length. Repeat until all the dough has been made into gnocchi. § Set a large pot of salted water over high heat to boil. The gnocchi should be cooked in 4 or 5 batches. When the water is boiling, lower the first batch (20-24 gnocchi) gently into the water. After a few minutes they will rise to the top. Leave them to bob about for about a minute or two, then scoop them out with a slotted spoon. Place on a heated serving dish. Repeat until all the gnocchi are cooked. § Put the gorgonzola and butter into a heavy-bottomed pan. Place over low heat and stir gently with a wooden spoon until the cheese and butter have melted. Add the cream and cook over medium low heat for 3-4 minutes, or until the cream has reduced and the sauce is thick and creamy. Season with salt and pepper. § Pour over the gnocchi on the serving dish. Sprinkle with parmesan and serve immediately.

■ INGREDIENTS

Gnocchi
- 1½ pounds boiling potatoes
- approximately 2 cups all-purpose flour

Sauce
- 6 ounces gorgonzola cheese
- ⅓ cup butter
- 1¼ cups fresh cream
- salt and freshly ground black pepper
- 8 tablespoons freshly grated parmesan cheese

Wine: a dry white (Corvo di Salaparuta)

Variations

– For richer gnocchi, add ⅔ cup melted butter and 3 eggs to the basic dough. Prepare as above. You may need a little more flour. This will make *Gnocchi alla piemontese* (Piedmont-style gnocchi).
– Add 30 shelled and chopped walnuts to the gorgonzola and butter before adding the cream.

Right:
Gnocchi di patate al gorgonzola

GNOCCHI: see recipe p. 106

SAUCE

• ½ quantity of béchamel
  sauce (see recipe p. 24)
• 2 cups coarsely chopped
  fontina cheese
• 1½ cups coarsely chopped
  gorgonzola cheese
• 1¼ cups mascarpone cheese
• 1 cup freshly grated
  parmesan cheese
• salt and freshly ground
  black pepper

GNOCCHI DI PATATE AI QUATTRO FORMAGGI
Potato gnocchi with four-cheese sauce

Serves: 6; Preparation: 20 minutes; Cooking: 30 minutes; Level of difficulty: Medium

Prepare the potato gnocchi. § Prepare the béchamel sauce. Add the four cheeses and stir over low heat until they have melted and the sauce is smooth and creamy. Season with salt and pepper. § Cook the gnocchi in a large pot of salted, boiling water following the instructions on the previous page. When all the gnocchi are cooked and laid out on a heated serving dish, pour the cheese sauce over the top and toss gently. Serve hot.

Gnocchi di patate e spinaci al burro e salvia
Potato and spinach gnocchi in butter and sage sauce

Serves: 6; Preparation: 20 minutes; Cooking: 50 minutes; Level of difficulty: Medium

Cook the potatoes in their skins in a pot of salted, boiling water for 20 minutes, or until tender. Drain and peel while hot. § Cook the spinach in a pot of salted water until tender (3-4 minutes if frozen, 8-10 minutes if fresh). Drain and squeeze out excess moisture. § Purée the potatoes and spinach together in a food mill. Place the mixture on a flat work surface. Work the eggs and flour in gradually. Add the nutmeg. Season with salt and pepper. Knead the mixture until smooth. § To prepare and cook the gnocchi, follow the instructions for potato gnocchi on p. 106. § When the gnocchi are cooked, quickly prepare the butter and sage sauce. Pour over the gnocchi and toss gently. Sprinkle with parmesan and serve hot.

■ INGREDIENTS

GNOCCHI
- 1 pound boiling potatoes
- 1 pound fresh or 11 ounces frozen spinach
- 2 eggs
- approximately ⅔ cup all-purpose flour
- ¼ cup butter
- dash of nutmeg
- salt and freshly ground black pepper
- 2 tablespoons freshly grated parmesan cheese

BUTTER AND SAGE SAUCE: see recipe p. 24

Wine: a dry red (Rosso dei vigneti del Brunello)

Gnocchi di spinaci e ricotta al pomodoro
Spinach and ricotta gnocchi in tomato and butter sauce

Serves: 6; Preparation: 45 minutes; Cooking: 25 minutes; Level of difficulty: Medium

Prepare the tomato and butter sauce. § Put the onion in a saucepan with the butter and sauté over medium heat until it turns golden brown. Remove the onion with a fork, leaving as much butter as possible in the pan. § Cook the spinach in a pot of salted water until tender (3-4 minutes if frozen, 8-10 minutes if fresh). Drain and squeeze out excess moisture. Chop finely. § Add the spinach to the pan with the butter. Sauté over medium-low heat for 10 minutes. Remove from heat and set aside. § When the spinach is cool, put it in a bowl with the ricotta, eggs, nutmeg, and all but 4 tablespoons of parmesan. Season with salt and pepper and mix well. Stir in the flour gradually until the dough is firm. § Lightly dust your hands with flour and roll pieces of dough into walnut-size balls. If the dough sticks to your hands, put it back into the bowl and add more flour. Place the gnocchi on a lightly floured platter. § Cook the gnocchi following the instructions on p. 106 for potato gnocchi. § Reheat the tomato sauce. Toss gently with the gnocchi. Sprinkle with the remaining parmesan and serve hot.

■ INGREDIENTS

TOMATO AND BUTTER SAUCE : see recipe p. 22

GNOCCHI
- 1 small onion, sliced in thin rings
- ¼ cup butter
- 1¾ pounds fresh or 1 pound frozen spinach
- ¾ cup fresh ricotta cheese
- 3 eggs
- dash of nutmeg
- 1½ cups freshly grated parmesan cheese
- salt and freshly ground black pepper
- approximately 2½ cups all-purpose flour

Wine: a dry red (Lambrusco)

Right:
Gnocchi di patate e spinaci al burro e salvia

Timballo di Gnocchi
Potato gnocchi in béchamel sauce baked in a pastry casing

Serves: 6; Preparation: 1 hour; Cooking: 1 hour; Level of difficulty: Complicated

Sift the flour into a mixing bowl with the eggs, lemon rind, and salt. Add the butter and mix well. When the dough is moist and firm but not sticky, roll it into a ball, cover with cling film, and place in the fridge for an hour. § Roll the dough out until it is about ⅜ inch thick. Grease the bottom and sides of a baking dish with butter and line with the dough. Prick well with a fork so that it doesn't swell while in the oven. § Bake in a preheated oven at 400° F for about 20 minutes, or until the pastry is golden brown. § Prepare and cook the potato gnocchi. § Prepare 1 quantity of béchamel sauce. § Put the cooked gnocchi in the béchamel and mix gently. Transfer to the baking dish with the pastry. Sprinkle with the parmesan cheese. Return to the oven and bake for 10 minutes more. Remove from the oven and slip the pastry casing containing the gnocchi out of the baking dish. Serve hot.

■ INGREDIENTS

GNOCCHI: see Potato gnocchi p. 106

PASTRY
- 2 cups all-purpose flour
- ½ cup butter
- 2 egg yolks
- finely grated rind of 1 lemon
- salt

BÉCHAMEL: see recipe p. 24

- 8 tablespoons freshly grated parmesan cheese
- ¼ cup butter

Wine: a dry red (Chianti delle Colline Pisane)

Gnocchi di Latte
Fried gnocchi

Serves: 4-6; Preparation: 50 minutes; Cooking: 40 minutes; Level of difficulty: Medium

Beat 5 egg yolks in a bowl with the sugar until smooth. § Place the potato flour in a heavy-bottomed pan. Stir the milk in gradually. Add the egg mixture, 2 tablespoons of the butter, nutmeg, cinnamon, and salt. Mix well with a wooden spoon. § Place the pan over medium heat and, stirring continually, bring to a boil. Boil for 10 minutes, stirring all the time. Remove from heat. § Turn the gnocchi batter out onto a flat work surface. Using a spatula dipped in cold water, spread it out to a thickness of about ½ inch and leave to cool for 30 minutes. § Cut the batter into ½-inch cubes. Beat the remaining egg in a bowl with a fork. Dust the gnocchi with flour, drop them into the beaten egg, then roll them in bread crumbs. § Fry the gnocchi in the remaining butter until they are golden brown. Place on a heated serving dish. Sprinkle with parmesan and serve immediately.

■ INGREDIENTS

- 1 egg and 5 egg yolks
- 1 tablespoon sugar
- ¾ cup potato flour
- 2 cups milk
- ⅔ cup butter
- ¼ teaspoon nutmeg
- ¼ teaspoon cinnamon
- salt
- 4 tablespoons all-purpose flour
- 6 tablespoons bread crumbs
- 8 tablespoons freshly grated parmesan cheese

Wine: a dry red (Collio Merlot)

Right:
Timballo di gnocchi
and *Gnocchi di latte*

GNOCCHI ALLA ROMANA
Baked semolina gnocchi

■ INGREDIENTS

- 1 quart milk
- 7 tablespoons butter
- 1¾ cups semolina
- 4 egg yolks
- 1 teaspoon salt
- 8 tablespoons freshly grated parmesan cheese
- 8 tablespoons freshly grated gruyère cheese

Wine: a medium red (Merlot di Aprilia)

Serves: 6; Preparation: 25 minutes; Cooking: 45 minutes; Level of difficulty: Medium

Put the milk and 1½ tablespoons of the butter in a heavy-bottomed pan and bring to a boil. Add the semolina very gradually just as the milk is beginning to boil. Stirring continually, cook over low heat for 15-20 minutes, or until the mixture is thick and no longer sticks to the sides of the pan. § Remove from heat and leave to cool for 2-3 minutes. Add the egg yolks, salt, 2 tablespoons of the parmesan and 2 tablespoons of the gruyère and mix well. § Wet a flat work surface with cold water and turn the gnocchi batter out onto it. Using a spatula dipped in cold water, spread it out to a thickness of about ½ inch. Leave the batter to cool to room temperature. § Use a cookie cutter or small glass with a diameter of about 1½-2 inches to cut the gnocchi into round disks. § Grease a baking dish with butter and place a row of gnocchi at one end. Lean the next row of gnocchi on the bottoms of the first, roof-tile fashion. Repeat until the baking dish is full. § Melt the remaining butter and pour over the gnocchi. Sprinkle with the remaining parmesan and gruyère. § Bake in a preheated oven at 400° F for about 20 minutes, or until a golden crust forms on top. Serve hot.

GNOCCHI ALLA BAVA
Baked potato gnocchi

■ INGREDIENTS

POTATO GNOCCHI: see recipe p. 106

SAUCE

- 8 ounces fontina cheese, sliced thinly
- ⅓ cup butter
- 8 tablespoons freshly grated parmesan cheese

Wine: a dry red (Barbaresco)

Serves: 6; Preparation: 25 minutes; Cooking: 40 minutes; Level of difficulty: Medium

Prepare and cook the potato gnocchi. Place them in a greased baking dish and cover with the sliced fontina. Dot with butter and sprinkle with the parmesan. § Bake in a preheated oven at 425° F for about 10 minutes, or until a golden crust has formed. Serve hot.

VARIATIONS
– Melt half the butter with a clove of finely chopped garlic and pour over the gnocchi before adding the cheese.
– Spinach and ricotta gnocchi can also be baked in the same way (see recipe p. 108).

Right:
Gnocchi alla romana

Soups and Salads

Satisfying and nourishing, hot pasta soups are lighter than most other pasta dishes. They are usually served with parmesan and a dash of oil. Pasta salads make great lunches, barbecue fillers, or starters for evening meals on hot summer nights.

Minestra di pasta e fagioli
Pasta and bean soup

Serves 4; Preparation: 5 minutes; Cooking 25 minutes + overnight soaking & cooking if using dried beans; Level of difficulty: Simple

Purée three-quarters of the beans in a food mill or blender. § Combine the onion and rosemary in a heavy-bottomed pan with the oil and sauté briefly over high heat. Before the onion begins to change color, add the puréed beans, tomato, and, if necessary, one or two cups of water. Season with salt and pepper and simmer over medium-low heat for about 15 minutes. § Add the pasta and remaining whole beans, and cook for 6-7 minutes, or until the pasta is cooked. Serve hot.

> VARIATION
> – For a heartier soup, add ½ cup finely chopped pancetta to the onion and rosemary mixture.

■ INGREDIENTS

• 1 pound white or red kidney beans, canned, or soaked and precooked as shown on the next page

• 1 small onion, finely chopped

• 1 tablespoon finely chopped fresh rosemary

• 4 tablespoons extra-virgin olive oil

• 1 ripe tomato, peeled and chopped

• salt and freshly ground black pepper

• 1⅓ cups mezzi rigatoni or other small, tubular pasta

Wine: a dry white
(Tocai di Lison)

Minestrone di verdura
Vegetable soup

This soup is a delicious and healthy appetizer for family dinners on cold winter evenings. Served at lunch with crunchy fresh bread, it is a meal-in-itself. In Tuscany, where the olive oil is particularly tasty, cooks add a dash of oil to each portion.

Serves 6; Preparation: 20 minutes + overnight soaking & cooking if using dried beans; Cooking 1 hour; Level of difficulty: Simple

Combine the celery, parsley, basil, onion, garlic, and carrot with the oil in a large, heavy-bottomed saucepan. Sauté for 2-3 minutes over medium heat. Add the cabbage and the carrot wheels. Sauté for another 2-3 minutes. Add the zucchini, peas, green beans, and boiling water. Simmer for 10 minutes. § Add the tomatoes and potatoes. Season with salt and pepper and simmer over medium-low heat for about 35 minutes, or until the vegetables are almost tender. § Add the chard leaves and stalks, kidney beans, and pasta and simmer for 7-8 minutes, or until the pasta is cooked *al dente*. Sprinkle with parmesan and serve hot.

■ INGREDIENTS

• 1 stalk celery, 1 tablespoon parsley, 4-5 fresh basil leaves, 1 medium onion, 1 clove garlic, 1 medium carrot, all finely chopped

• 4 tablespoons extra-virgin olive oil

• 8 ounces savoy cabbage, chopped in thin strips

• 1 carrot, sliced in wheels

• 2 small zucchini, diced

• 1⅓ cups fresh or frozen peas

• 1¼ cups sliced green beans

• 2 quarts boiling water

• 2 large tomatoes, peeled and chopped

Right:
Minestrone di verdura

- 2 medium potatoes, diced
- salt and freshly ground black pepper
- 1½ cups fresh chard, torn
- ¾ cup white kidney beans, canned, or soaked and precooked as shown here
- 2 tablespoons freshly grated parmesan cheese
- 1⅓ cups soup pasta

Wine: a young, dry red
(Vino Novello)

SOAKING AND COOKING BEANS

If you have the time, dried beans soaked overnight and precooked will make both these soups more appetizing than if you use the bland and pulpy canned varieties.

Place the beans in a large bowl with at least 3 inches of water over the top. Cover with a dishcloth and leave overnight. § Drain and rinse well under cold water. Place in a large pot of cold water, cover, and bring to a boil over medium heat. § Simmer over low heat for about 50 minutes, or until the beans are tender but not mushy. Add salt about 10 minutes before the beans are cooked.

Insalata di ruote con le verdure
Ruote salad with vegetables

Serves 4; Preparation: 15 minutes; Cooking 15 minutes; Level of difficulty: Simple

Cook the ruote in a large pot of salted, boiling water until *al dente*. Drain thoroughly. Transfer to a large salad bowl and toss vigorously with half the oil. Set aside to cool. § Cut the stalk and hard base off the eggplant and peel. Cut crosswise into slices about ½-inch thick. Place the slices under the broiler and broil for about 10 minutes, or until tender. Dice the cooked slices in ¾-inch squares. § Quarter the bell peppers lengthwise and slice each quarter into thin strips. Slice the white, bottom part of the scallion very finely. § Combine the remaining oil, capers, oregano, parsley, eggplant, bell peppers, and pecorino with the pasta. Sprinkle with salt and pepper. Make sure the salad is completely cool before serving.

■ INGREDIENTS

- 6 tablespoons extra-virgin olive oil
- 1 large eggplant
- 1 large yellow and 1 large red bell pepper
- 2 scallions
- 2½ tablespoons capers
- 1 teaspoon dried oregano
- 2 tablespoons finely chopped parsley
- 3 tablespoons freshly grated pecorino cheese
- salt and freshly ground black pepper
- 14 ounces ruote, plain, whole wheat or colored

Wine: a dry, young white (Frascati)

Insalata di fusilli con pomodori, aglio e mozzarella
Fusilli salad with tomato, garlic, and mozzarella cheese

Serves 4; Preparation: 10 minutes; Cooking 10 minutes; Level of difficulty: Simple

Cook the fusilli in a large pot of salted, boiling water until *al dente*. Drain well. Transfer to a large salad bowl and toss vigorously with half the oil. Set aside to cool. § Cut the tomatoes into bite-size pieces and add to the pasta. Combine the garlic and parsley with the remainder of the oil and a sprinkling of salt, and add to the salad bowl. Leave to cool completely. § Just before serving, dice the mozzarella into ½-inch cubes on a cutting board. Slant the board slightly so that the extra liquid runs off. Sprinkle over the top of the salad with the torn basil leaves and freshly ground black pepper. Serve cool.

■ INGREDIENTS

- salt and freshly ground black pepper
- 4 tablespoons extra-virgin olive oil
- 4 large ripe tomatoes
- 2 cloves garlic, finely chopped
- 2 tablespoons finely chopped parsley
- 12 ounces mozzarella cheese
- 6 fresh basil leaves
- 14 ounces fusilli, plain, whole wheat or colored

Wine: a dry white (Colonna)

VARIATION
– Add 1 tablespoon mustard to the oil for a sharper flavor.

Right:
Insalata di ruote con le verdure
and *Insalata di fusilli con pomodori*

INGREDIENTS

- salt
- 4 tablespoons extra-virgin olive oil
- 4 hard-cooked eggs
- 3 large ripe tomatoes
- 7 ounces tuna, preserved in oil
- 2 scallions
- 4 tablespoons mayonnaise
- 2 tablespoons finely chopped parsley
- 14 ounces conchiglie

INSALATA DI CONCHIGLIE SPLENDIDA
Conchiglie with eggs, tomato, tuna, onion and mayonnaise

Serves 4; Preparation: 5 minutes; Cooking 12 minutes; Level of difficulty: Simple

Cook the conchiglie in a large pot of salted, boiling water until *al dente*. Drain very thoroughly. Transfer to a large salad bowl and toss well with half the oil. Set aside to cool. § Peel the eggs and cut into quarters lengthwise. Dice the tomatoes into bite-sized cubes. Break the tuna up by lightly pressing with a fork. Slice the white, bottom part of the scallion thinly. § When the pasta is cool, add the eggs, tomatoes, tuna, parsley, remaining oil, and mayonnaise. Sprinkle with salt, mix well, and serve.

Making Fresh Pasta at Home

Fresh pasta can be made either by hand or using a pasta machine. I strongly advise you not to use the pasta machines that mix the dough as well as cutting the pasta, since the finished product will be heavy and very inferior to handmade pasta. Thus the first step in pasta making is to prepare the dough.

Mixing plain pasta dough

For 4 generous servings you will need 3 cups of all-purpose flour and 3 medium eggs. Place the flour in a mound on a flat work surface and hollow out a well in the center. Break the eggs into the well one by one and beat lightly with a fork for 1-2 minutes. Pull some of the surrounding flour down over the egg mixture and gradually incorporate it. Continue until the mixture is no longer runny. Using your hands now, combine all the flour with the eggs. Work the mixture with your hands until it is smooth and moist, but quite firm.

To test the mixture for the correct consistency, press a clean finger into the dough. If it comes out easily and without any dough sticking to it, it is ready for kneading. If it is too moist, add more flour. If it is too dry, incorporate a little milk. Roll the mixture into a ball shape.

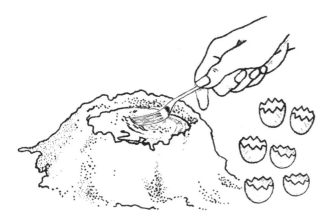 

Mixing spinach pasta dough

For 4 generous servings you will need 2 cups of all-purpose flour, 3 cups of fresh spinach (or 1 cup thawed frozen spinach) and 2 large eggs. Cook the spinach in a little salted water until tender. Drain well and, when cool, squeeze out any excess moisture. Chop finely with a knife. Proceed as above for plain flour dough, working the spinach in together with the eggs.

KNEADING THE DOUGH

Clean the work surface of any excess dough or flour and lightly sprinkle with all-purpose flour. Push down and forwards on the ball of pasta dough with the heel of your palm. Fold the slightly extended piece of dough in half, give it a quarter-turn, and repeat the process. Continue for about 10 minutes or until the dough is very smooth. Place the ball of pasta dough on a plate and cover with an upturned bowl. Leave to rest for at least 15-20 minutes.

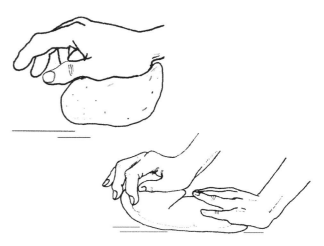

ROLLING THE DOUGH OUT BY HAND

Place the ball of dough on a flat, clean work surface and flatten it a little with your hand. Place the rolling pin on the center of the flattened ball and, applying light but firm pressure, roll the dough away from you. Give the ball a quarter-turn and repeat. When the dough has become a large round about ¼ inch thick, curl the far edge over the pin while holding the edge closest to you with your hand. Gently stretch the pasta as you roll it all onto the pin. Unroll, give the dough a quarter-turn, and repeat. Continue rolling and stretching the dough until it is transparent.

ROLLING THE DOUGH OUT USING THE PASTA MACHINE

Divide the dough in to several pieces and flatten them slightly with your hand. Set the machine with its rollers at their widest, and run each piece through the machine. Reduce the rollers' width by one notch and repeat, reducing the rollers' width by one notch each time. Continue until all the pieces have gone through the machine at the thinnest roller setting.

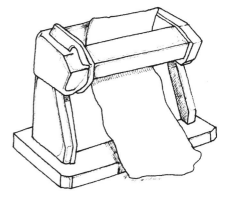

CUTTING THE PASTA BY HAND

For lasagna: cut the rolled out pasta into oblongs sheets about 3 inches wide and 12 inches long.

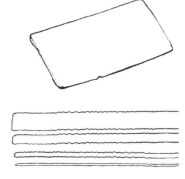

For tagliolini, fettuccine, tagliatelle, and pappardelle: fold the hand-rolled pasta into a loose, flat roll. Using a large sharp knife, cut the roll into ⅛-inch slices (for tagliolini), ¼-inch slices (for fettuccine), ⅓-inch slices (for tagliatelle), or ¾-inch slices (for pappardelle). Unravel the pasta and lay it out flat on a clean dishcloth. If you want fluted edges, use the wheel cutter on the pasta laid out flat. You will need a steady hand!

For maltagliati: fold the hand-rolled pasta into a loose, flat roll. Using a large sharp knife cut the pasta into rhomboid shapes. Separate the pieces and lay them out on a clean dishcloth.

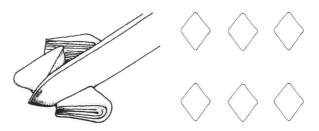

CUTTING THE PASTA BY MACHINE

Cut the pieces of pasta lengthwise so that they are about 12 inches long. Attach the cutters to the pasta machine and set the machine at the widths given above for the various types of pasta. Lay the cut pasta out on clean dry dishcloths.

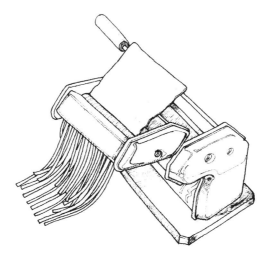

MAKING STUFFED PASTA

Pasta dough for stuffed pasta needs to be fairly moist, so try to work quickly and keep all the dough you are not using on a plate under an upturned dish.

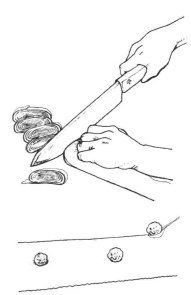

For agnolotti, tortelli, and square-shaped ravioli: these are the easiest filled pasta shapes to make. Using a large sharp knife, cut the rolled out pasta into strips about 4 inches wide. Place heaped teaspoonfuls of the mixture for the filling at intervals of about 2 inches down the middle. Slightly moisten the edges of the pasta with your fingertips before folding them over and sealing them. Use a wheel cutter to cut between the stuffing. Run it along the sealed edges to give them a decorative, fluted edge as well.

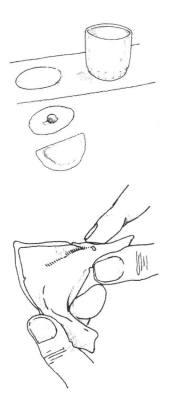

For half-moon shaped ravioli: use a glass or cookie cutter to cut the rolled out pasta into circular shapes. Place a teaspoonful of the filling at the center, moisten the edges of the pasta with your fingertips and fold it over. Pinch the edges toegther with your fingers until they are well sealed. For fluted edges, run round each shape with the pastry cutter.

For tortellini: use a glass or cookie cutter to cut the rolled out pasta into circular shapes. Place ½ teaspoonful of the filling mixture in the middle of each round. Moisten the edges of the pasta with your fingertips and fold the pasta over. Pick the tortellino up and twist it around your index finger until the edges meet. Pinch them together with your fingers and seal them.

For tortelloni: as above, but using a much larger glass or a small bowl (3½ inches in diameter) and 1 teaspoonful of the filling mixture.

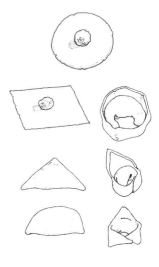

For cappelletti: using a large sharp knife, cut the rolled out pasta into strips about 2 inches wide. Cut each strip into 2-inch squares. Place ½ teaspoonfuls of the filling mixture in the center of each. Fold the square diagonally in half to form a triangle. Moisten the edges slightly with your fingertips and seal them together. Pick up the triangle by one corner of its folded over side. Take the other folded over corner and wrap it around your index finger. Pinch the edges together to seal the pasta.

Index

Acini di pepe 11
agnolini
~ with chicken filling in chicken
  broth 88, 89
agnolotti 12
~ in meat broth 80, 81
~ with meat sauce 80
amatriciana
~ bucatini all'amatriciana 41
anelli rigati 11
anellini 11
arrabbiata
~ penne all'arrabbiata 44
artichokes
~ penne with artichokes 44, 45
asparagus
~ penne with asparagus 61

Baked pasta 92-103
Basic sauces 22-36
basil 19
~ Genoese basil sauce 28, 29
~ Tuscan-style pesto 28
bavette 10
~ with green beans, potatoes
  and pesto 60
bay leaf 18
beans
~ pasta and bean soup 116, 117
béchamel sauce 24, 25
~ cannelloni with ricotta and
  spinach filling in tomato and
  béchamel sauce 96, 97
~ maccheroni with meat sauce,
  béchamel and truffles baked
  in pastry casing 100
~ potato gnocchi in béchamel
  sauce in a pastry casing 110,
  111
black pepper 18
Bolognese meat sauce 26, 27
~ lasagne with Bolognese meat
  sauce 94
bread crumbs
~ spaghetti with onion, garlic
  and bread crumbs 62

broccoli
~ festonati with Italian sausages
  and broccoli 46, 47
broth
~ agnolini with chicken filling
  in chicken broth 88, 89
~ agnolotti in meat broth 80, 81
~ fish broth 34
~ meat broth 34, 35
bucatini 10
~ with capers and black olives 40
~ with pancetta and spicy
  tomato sauce 41
bucatoni 10
~ with onion sauce 54
butter
~ butter and parmesan sauce 24
~ butter and sage sauce 24
~ fettuccine with butter and
  cream sauce 77
~ fettuccine with simple butter
  and tomato sauce 74, 75
~ ravioli with Italian sausage
  filling in butter sauce 82, 83
~ ravioli with ricotta filling in
  butter and sage sauce 83
~ ravioli with zucchini filling in
  butter and rosemary sauce 88
~ spinach and ricotta gnocchi in
  tomato and butter sauce 108
~ tomato and butter sauce 22
~ tortelli with potato filling in
  butter and sage sauce 86
~ tortelli with chard filling in
  butter and parmesan sauce
  86-87

Cannaroni lisci 11
cannelloni
~ with ricotta and spinach
  filling in tomato and
  béchamel sauce 96, 97
capelli d'angelo 10
~ with oil and lemon sauce 42, 43
capers 18
~ bucatini with capers and
  black olives 40
cappelletti 12

carbonara
~ spaghetti alla carbonara 38, 39
carrettiera
~ spaghetti alla carrettiera 62
cauliflower
~ conchiglie with cauliflower,
  garlic and chilies 56, 57
cavatappi 11
chard
~ orecchiette with chard 60, 61
~ tortelli with chard filling in
  butter and parmesan sauce
  86-87
cheese 16-17
~ potato gnocchi with four-
  cheese sauce 107
~ tortelloni with veal, spinach
  and rosemary filling in cheese
  sauce 90-91
chicken
~ agnolini with chicken filling
  in chicken broth 88, 89
~ tagliatelle with chicken-liver
  sauce 76
chilies 18
~ bucatini with pancetta and
  spicy tomato sauce 41
~ conchiglie with cauliflower,
  garlic and chilies 56, 57
~ penne with "angry" tomato
  sauce 44
~ spaghettini with oil, garlic
  and chilies 38
~ spaghettini with spicy tomato
  sauce 40
clams
~ spaghetti with clams 48, 49
~ spaghetti with shellfish sauce 48
~ tagliatelle with clams and
  cream 66
colander 20
conchiglie
~ with cauliflower, garlic and
  chilies 56, 57
~ with eggs, tomato, tuna,
  onion and mayonnaise 119
conchigliette 11
conchigline 11

conchiglione 11
cream
~ baked maltagliati with ham, cream and eggs 102
~ fettuccine with butter and cream sauce 77
~ paglia e fieno with cream and truffles 70
~ spinach tagliatelle with fresh cream, peas and gorgonzola cheese 72, 73
~ tagliatelle with clams and cream 66
~ tortellini with cream sauce 84, 85
curry
~ tagliolini with curry sauce 71
cuttlefish
~ spaghetti with cuttlefish 50

Ditali rigati 11
ditaloni rigati 11
~ baked tomatoes with pasta filling 102-103
Dried pasta 36-63
duck
~ tagliatelle with duck sauce 76, 77

Eggs
~ baked maltagliati with ham, cream and eggs 102
~ conchiglie with eggs, tomato, tuna, onion and mayonnaise 119
~ fried gnocchi 110, 111
~ maccheroni baked with veal, salame, eggs, mozzarella cheese and vegetables 98
~ spaghetti with eggs and pancetta 38, 39
eggplants
~ spaghetti with fried eggplants 58

False "meat" sauce 32
farfalle 11
~ with peas and ham 55
~ with salmon and vodka sauce 49
farfalline 11
fava beans
~ linguine with fava beans and

fresh rosemary 50, 51
fedelini rigati 11
festonati 11
~ with Italian sausages and broccoli 46, 47
fettuccine 13
~ with butter and cream sauce 77
figurine 11
Filled pasta 12-13, 79-91
fish
~ fish broth 34
~ fish sauce 32, 33
~ ravioli with fish filling in vegetable sauce 90, 91
fontina 17
Fresh pasta 12-13, 64-77
fusilli 10, 11
~ salad with tomato, garlic and mozzarella cheese 118, 119
~ with tomato and mozzarella cheese 52, 53
fusilli
~ with tomatoes and mozzarella cheese 97
fusilli bucati 11
fusilli lunghi
~ with leeks 62, 63

Garlic 18
~ conchiglie with cauliflower, garlic and chilies 56, 57
~ fusilli salad with tomato, garlic and mozzarella cheese 118, 119
~ penne with fresh tomatoes, garlic and mozzarella cheese 43
~ spaghetti with onion, garlic and bread crumbs 62
~ spaghettini with garlic, oil and chilies 38
gemelli 11
Genoese basil sauce 28, 29
gnocchi (dried) 11
Gnocchi (fresh) 14, 104-113
~ baked semolina gnocchi 112, 113
~ baked potato gnocchi 112
~ fried gnocchi 110, 111
~ gnocchi alla romana 14
~ potato and spinach gnocchi in butter and sage sauce 108, 109
~ potato gnocchi 14
~ potato gnocchi in béchamel sauce in a pastry casing 110, 111

~ potato gnocchi with four-cheese sauce 107
~ potato gnocchi with gorgonzola cheese sauce 106, 107
~ spinach and potato gnocchi 14
gnocchi
~ spinach and ricotta gnocchi in tomato and butter sauce 108
gorgonzola 17
~ potato gnocchi with gorgonzola cheese sauce 106, 107
~ spinach tagliatelle with fresh cream, peas and gorgonzola cheese 72, 73
green beans
~ bavette with green beans, potatoes and pesto 60

Ham 16
~ baked maltagliati with ham, cream and eggs 102
~ farfalle with peas and ham 55
~ Tuscan style paglia e fieno 70, 71
Herbs and spices 18-19

Lagane 8
lamb
~ maltagliati with lamb sauce 73
lasagne 13
~ with Bolognese meat sauce 94
leeks
~ fusilli lunghi with leeks 62, 63
lemon
~ capelli d'angelo with oil and lemon sauce 42, 43
~ penne with artichokes 44, 45
linguine 10
~ with fava beans and fresh rosemary 50, 51
~ with pesto 29
Long pasta 10
lumaconi
~ with vegetables 56, 57
lumaconi rigati 11

Maccheroni 11
~ baked with veal, salame, eggs, mozzarella cheese and vegetables 98
~ maccheroni with fish sauce 33
~ with meat sauce, béchamel

and truffles baked in pastry
casing 100
~ with peppers 53
maggiorana 19
malfatti 14
malloreddus 11
~ with Italian sausages and
pecorino cheese 58, 59
maltagliati 13
~ baked maltagliati with ham,
cream and eggs 102
~ with lamb sauce 73
marjoram 19
mascarpone
~ tagliolini with mascarpone
cheese sauce 66, 67
mayonnaise
~ conchiglie with eggs, tomato,
tuna, onion and mayonnaise
119
meat broth 34, 35
~ agnolotti in meat broth 80, 81
meat sauce
~ agnolotti with meat sauce 80
~ Bolognese meat sauce 26, 27
~ lasagne with Bolognese meat
sauce 94
~ maccheroni with meat sauce,
béchamel and truffles baked
in pastry casing 100
~ quick meat sauce 26
~ rigatoni giganti filled with
meat sauce 94-95
mezzi rigatoni 11
~ pasta and bean soup 116
milk
~ fried gnocchi 110, 111
millerighe 11
minestre 11
minestrone 116-117
mortadella 16
mozzarella 17
~ baked penne rigate 98, 99
mozzarella
~ fusilli salad with tomato,
garlic and mozzarella cheese
118, 119
~ fusilli with tomato and
mozzarella cheese 52, 53, 97
~ maccheroni baked with veal,
salame, eggs, mozzarella
cheese and vegetables 98
~ penne with fresh tomatoes,
garlic and mozzarella cheese 43

mushrooms
~ Italian mushroom sauce 30, 31
~ tagliatelle with olives and
mushrooms 74
mushrooms
~ tortellini with woodsmen-
style sauce 84, 85
mussels
~ spaghetti with shellfish sauce 48

Noce moscata 18
Norma
~ spaghetti alla Norma 58
nutmeg 18

Olive oil 16
~ capelli d'angelo with oil and
lemon sauce 42, 43
~ spaghettini with garlic, oil
and chilies 38
olives
~ bucatini with capers and
black olives 40
~ tagliatelle with olives and
mushrooms 74
onion
~ conchiglie with eggs, tomato,
tuna, onion and mayonnaise
119
~ bucatoni with onion sauce 54
~ spaghetti with onion, garlic
and bread crumbs 62
orecchiette 11
~ with chard 60, 61
oregano 18

Paglia e fieno 13
~ with cream and truffles 70
~ Tuscan style paglia e fieno 70,
71
pancetta 16
~ bucatini with pancetta and
spicy tomato sauce 41
~ false "meat" sauce 32
~ tagliatelle with crispy fried
pancetta 69
~ Tuscan style paglia e fieno 70, 71
pappardelle 13
~ with wild hare sauce 68, 69

parmesan
~ butter and parmesan sauce 24
~ tortelli with chard filling in
butter and parmesan sauce 86-87
parmigiano 17
parsley 19
Pasta
~ al dente 21
~ cooking pasta 21
~ cutting pasta by hand 122
~ cutting pasta by machine 122
~ draining pasta 21
~ History of pasta 8-9
~ kneading pasta dough 121
~ making fresh pasta at home
120-123
~ pasta dough 120
~ quantities 21
~ rolling pasta dough by hand
121
~ rolling pasta dough with a
pasta machine 121
~ salt for pasta cooking 21
~ serving pasta 21
~ serving suggestions for fresh
and filled pasta 13
~ spinach pasta dough 120
pasta
~ stuffed pasta 123
~ tips for cooking pasta 21
~ water for pasta cooking 21
pasta e fagioli 116
Pasta salads 114-119
Pasta soups 114-119
pasticcio 102
pastine 11
pastry
~ maccheroni with meat sauce,
béchamel and truffles baked
in pastry casing 100
~ potato gnocchi in béchamel
sauce in a pastry casing 110,
111
peas
~ farfalle with peas and ham 55
~ spinach tagliatelle with fresh
cream, peas and gorgonzola
cheese 72, 73
pecorino 17
~ baked penne rigate 98, 99
~ malloreddus with Italian
sausages and pecorino cheese
58, 59
penne

~ with artichokes 44, **45**
~ with asparagus 61
~ with fresh tomatoes, garlic
    and mozzarella cheese 43
penne
~ with ricotta cheese 45
penne lisce 11
penne rigate
~ baked penne rigate 98, **99**
peppers
~ maccheroni with peppers 53
pesto 28, **29**
~ bavette with green beans,
    potatoes and pesto 60
pipette rigate 11
plain conchiglie 11
plain eliche 11
plain penne rigate 11
porcini 30, 31
~ Italian mushroom sauce 30, 31
pot 20
potatoes
~ baked potato gnocchi 112
~ bavette with green beans,
    potatoes and pesto 60
~ potato and spinach gnocchi
    in butter and sage sauce 108,
    109
~ potato gnocchi in béchamel
    sauce in a pastry casing 110,
    111
~ potato gnocchi with four-
    cheese sauce 107
~ potato gnocchi with
    gorgonzola cheese sauce 106,
    107
~ tortelli with potato filling in
    butter and sage sauce 86
prosciutto 16
~ tagliatelle with prosciutto 68
puttanesca
~ spaghettini alla puttanesca 40

Quadrucci 11
quick meat sauce 26

Ragù 26, **27**
ragù di pesce 32, **33**
ravioli
~ with fish filling in vegetable
    sauce 90, **91**

~ with Italian sausage filling in
    butter sauce 82, **83**
~ with ricotta filling in butter
    and sage sauce 83
~ with zucchini filling in butter
    and rosemary sauce 88
ricotta 17
~ baked spinach and ricotta roll
    100-101
~ cannelloni with ricotta and
    spinach filling in tomato and
    béchamel sauce 96, 97
~ penne with ricotta cheese 45
~ ravioli with ricotta filling in
    butter and sage sauce 83
~ spinach and ricotta gnocchi
    in tomato and butter sauce
    108
~ spinach ravioli with ricotta
    cheese filling in tomato sauce
    82
rigatoni 11
~ with zucchini 46
rigatoni giganti
~ filled with meat sauce 94-95
rigatoni napoletani 11
rosemary 19
~ linguine with broad beans
    and fresh rosemary 50, **51**
~ ravioli with zucchini filling in
    butter and rosemary sauce 88
~ tortelloni with veal, spinach
    and rosemary filling in cheese
    sauce 90-91
ruote 11
~ salad with vegetables 118, **119**

Sage 19
~ butter and sage sauce 24
~ potato and spinach gnocchi
    in butter and sage sauce 108,
    109
~ ravioli with ricotta filling in
    butter and sage sauce 83
~ tortelli with potato filling in
    butter and sage sauce 86
salame
~ maccheroni baked with veal,
    salame, eggs, mozzarella
    cheese and vegetables 98
salmon
~ farfalle with salmon and
    vodka sauce 49

sausages
~ festonati with Italian sausages
    and broccoli 46, **47**
~ malloreddus with Italian
    sausages and pecorino cheese
    58, **59**
sausages
~ ravioli with Italian sausage
    filling in butter sauce 82, **83**
semolina
~ baked semolina gnocchi 112,
    113
shellfish
~ spaghetti with shellfish sauce
    48
Short pasta 10
Soup pasta 11
~ vegetable soup 116-118
spaghetti 10
~ with clams 48, **49**
~ with cuttlefish 50
~ with eggs and pancetta 38, **39**
~ with fried eggplants 58
~ with onion, garlic and bread
    crumbs 62
~ with shellfish sauce 48
~ with simple tomato sauce **23**
spaghettini 10
~ with garlic, oil and chilies 38
~ with spicy tomato sauce 40
~ with tuna and tomato sauce
    54
Special pasta 15
spinach
~ baked spinach and ricotta roll
    100-101
spinach
~ cannelloni with ricotta and
    spinach filling in tomato and
    béchamel sauce 96, 97
~ potato and spinach gnocchi
    in butter and sage sauce 108,
    109
~ spinach and ricotta gnocchi
    in tomato and butter sauce
    108
~ tortelloni with veal, spinach
    and rosemary filling in cheese
    sauce 90-91
spinach conchiglie 11
spinach eliche 11
spinach penne rigate 11
spinach ravioli 12
~ with ricotta cheese filling in

tomato sauce 82
spinach spaghetti 10
spinach tagliatelle
~ with fresh cream, peas and gorgonzola cheese 72, 73
stelline 11
strudel 100-101
sugar
~ fried gnocchi 110, 111
sugo finto 32

T

Tagliatelle 13
~ with duck sauce 76, 77
~ with chicken-liver sauce 76
~ with clams and cream 66
~ with crispy fried pancetta 69
~ with olives and mushrooms 74
~ with prosciutto 68
~ with simple butter and tomato sauce 74, 75
tagliolini 13
~ with curry sauce 71
~ with Italian mushroom sauce 31
~ with mascarpone cheese sauce 66, 67
timballo 100, 110
tomato
~ "angry" tomato sauce 44
~ baked tomatoes with pasta filling 102-103
~ bucatini with pancetta and spicy tomato sauce 41
~ cannelloni with ricotta and spinach filling in tomato and béchamel sauce 96, 97
~ conchiglie with eggs, tomato, tuna, onion and mayonnaise 119
tomato
~ fusilli salad with tomato, garlic and mozzarella cheese 118, 119
~ fusilli with tomato and mozzarella cheese 52, 53, 97
~ penne with "angry" tomato sauce 44
~ penne with fresh tomatoes, garlic and mozzarella cheese 43
~ simple tomato sauce 22, 23
~ spaghettini with spicy tomato

sauce 40
tomato
~ spinach and ricotta gnocchi in tomato and butter sauce 108
~ spinach ravioli with ricotta cheese filling in tomato sauce 82
~ tagliatelle with simple butter and tomato sauce 74, 75
~ tomato and butter sauce 22
tomato conchiglie 11
tomato eliche 11
tomato spaghetti 10
topini 14
tortelli 12
~ with potato filling in butter and sage sauce 86
~ with chard filling in butter and parmesan sauce 86-87
tortellini 12
~ with bolognese meat sauce 27
~ with cream sauce 84, 85
~ with woodsmen-style sauce 84, 85
tortelloni 12
~ with veal, spinach and
tortelloni
~ rosemary filling in cheese sauce 90-91
tripolini 11
truffles
~ maccheroni with meat sauce, béchamel and truffles baked in pastry casing 100
~ paglia e fieno with cream and truffles 70
tuna
~ conchiglie with eggs, tomato, tuna, onion and mayonnaise 119
~ spaghettini with tuna and tomato sauce 54
Tuscan-style paglia e fieno 70, 71
Tuscan-style pesto 28

U

Utensils for making and cooking pasta 20-21
~ baking dish 21
~ cheese grater 21

utensils
~ cutting board 20
~ food mill 21
~ food processor 21
~ measuring cup 21
~ metal tongs 20
~ pasta machine 20
~ rolling pin 21
~ saucepan 20
~ sauté pan 20
~ skillet 20
~ slotted spoon 21
~ wheel cutter 20
~ wooden fork 20
~ wooden spoon 20

V

Veal
~ maccheroni baked with veal, salame, eggs, mozzarella cheese and vegetables 98
~ tortelloni with veal, spinach and rosemary filling in cheese sauce 90-91
vegetable soup 116-118
vegetables
~ lumaconi with vegetables 56, 57
~ maccheroni baked with veal, salame, eggs, mozzarella cheese and vegetables 98
~ ravioli with fish filling in vegetable sauce 90, 91
~ ruote salad with vegetables 118, 119
vodka
~ farfalle with salmon and vodka sauce 49

W

Walnut sauce 30
whole wheat rigatoni 11
wild hare
~ pappardelle with wild hare sauce 68, 69
wine 16

Z

Zucchini
~ ravioli with zucchini filling in butter and rosemary sauce 88
~ rigatoni with zucchini 46